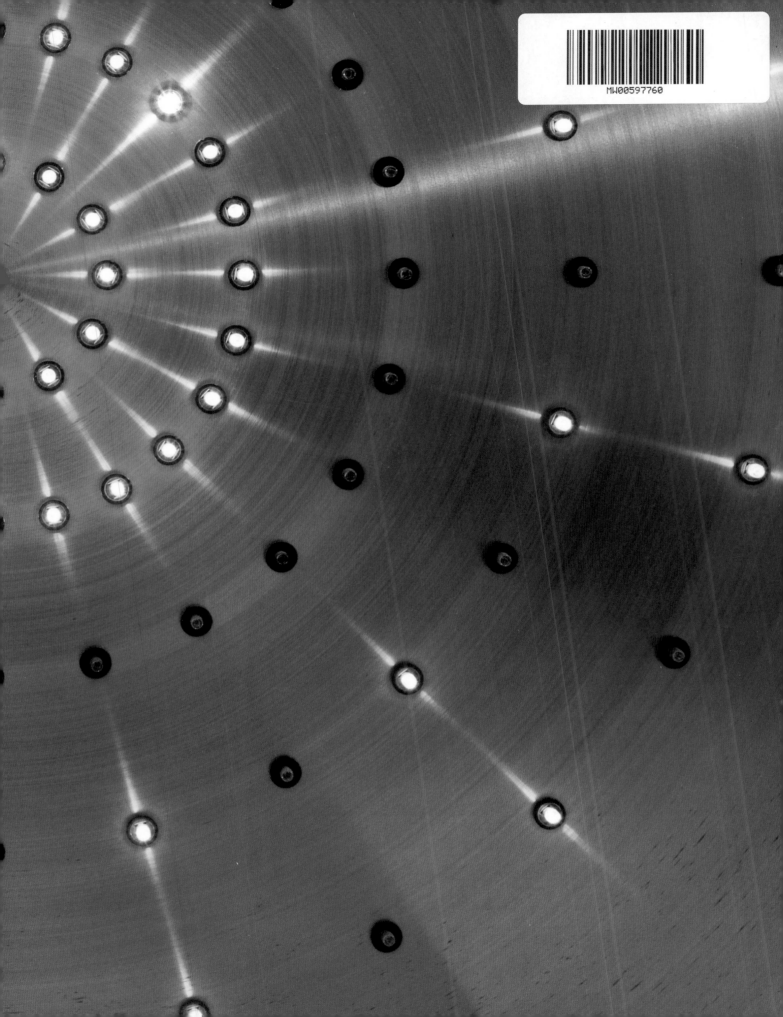

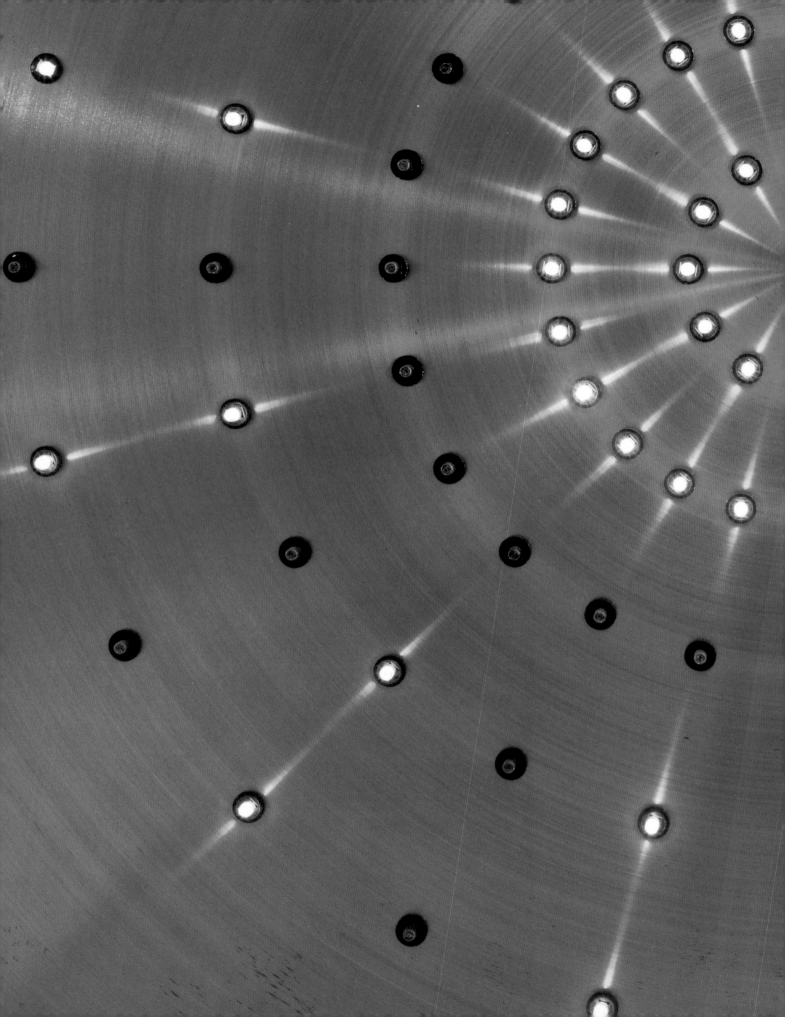

The Age of Independent Advice

THE REMARKABLE HISTORY
of the Independent Registered Investment Adviser Industry

Published by The Charles Schwab Corporation, San Francisco, California

Mutual Fund OneSource, Mutual Fund Marketplace, Schwab Institutional, SchwabLink, Schwab Performance Technologies and Charles R. Schwab Impact Awards are registered trademarks or trademarks of Charles Schwab & Co., Inc. used with permission.

Certified Financial Planner Board of Standards, Inc. owns the certification marks CFP®, Certified Financial Planner™ and federally registered CFP (with flame design) in the U.S., which it awards to individuals who successfully complete CFP Board's initial and ongoing certification requirements.
Financial Planning Standards Board Ltd. owns the CFP®, Certified Financial Planner™ and CFP (with flame design) marks outside the U.S. and its territories.

Cover and text designed by Seventeenth Street Studios

Printed in Canada

ISBN 978-0-9796227-0-0

10 9 8 7 6 5 4 3 2 1

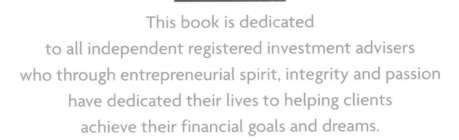

This book is dedicated
to all independent registered investment advisers
who through entrepreneurial spirit, integrity and passion
have dedicated their lives to helping clients
achieve their financial goals and dreams.

Contents

Foreword

THIS BOOK SERVES A DUAL PURPOSE. Not only does it chronicle the remarkable evolution of one of the fastest growing parts of the financial services world, but even more important, it captures the vision and spirit that have nurtured that growth.

I feel especially close to the independent registered investment adviser industry because of my personal history. While Schwab began as a pure "discount broker," my own roots lie in the investment advisory business. The lessons I learned in those early years working as a securities analyst and portfolio manager—including the most important lesson, the importance of ethical, objective advice—have remained central to my life's work.

Not coincidentally, in many ways Schwab and the registered investment adviser industry have grown up together. Bound by the belief that the investor must come first, and that we could offer a better alternative to Wall Street's business as usual, we both have forged new ground while enjoying decades of unprecedented growth. There is no question in my mind that our successes would not have been possible if we had not remained true to this mission.

Therefore, as we at Schwab celebrate the twentieth anniversary of Schwab Institutional in 2007, we are honored to have been able to support the growth of independent advisers, who have helped revolutionize the financial services industry.

I hope this book not only helps us look back and appreciate the contributions of the many talented and committed people who have guided this success, but that it will also instill us with a renewed sense of excitement for the future.

At its core, this book is a celebration of the registered investment adviser business—and by extension, a celebration of the American investor. Schwab and Schwab Institutional pledge to remain committed to our mission to helping more Americans become successful investors. This is truly a remarkable history, and we can all look to it for inspiration.

Charles R. Schwab
Chairman and Chief Executive Officer
The Charles Schwab Corporation

Acknowledgments

INDEPENDENT REGISTERED investment advisers represent more than an industry. They're a true community of smart, ethical, passionate, talented, and dedicated individuals driven by a desire to help their clients achieve their financial and life goals. It's that community, and those qualities, that we honor in this book.

Deborah Doyle McWhinney and Charles Goldman of Schwab Institutional share the original vision for chronicling the history of this extraordinary industry, but their vision could not have been realized without the generous support of independent advisers and the many people who work with them. Thanks go to all those who shared their time, stories, resources, knowledge, and expertise to help bring this book to life.

We wish first to thank the more than 5,000 advisers whom Schwab Institutional has the privilege to serve. We appreciate your business and thank you for entrusting Schwab with your clients' assets.

We gratefully acknowledge the advisers who agreed to be interviewed and made themselves available as the manuscript was being developed:

Elaine Bedel, Bedel Financial Consulting; David Bugen, Regent Atlantic Capital; Harold Evensky, Evensky & Katz Wealth Management; Fred Fern and Randy Conner, Churchill Management Group; Ken Fisher, Fisher Investments; Gary Furukawa, Freestone Capital Management; Roger Hewins, Hewins Financial Advisors; Rick Keller, The Keller Group Investment Management; Tim Kochis, Kochis Fitz Wealth Management; Doug Lane, Douglas C. Lane & Associates; Steve Lockshin, Convergent Wealth Advisors; Mary A. Malgoire, The Family Firm, Inc.; Peggy Ruhlin, Budros, Ruhlin & Roe; Joe Sheehan, Moneta Group; Howard Sontag, Sontag Advisory; Rich Steinberg, Steinberg Global Asset Management; Deb Wetherby, Wetherby Asset Management; and Dale Yahnke, Dowling & Yahnke, Inc.

This book could not have written without the help of many industry experts, clients, and scholars who provided research materials and generously shared their time and knowledge with us:

Dr. William Anthes, former president of the College for Financial Planning and retired chief executive officer of the National Endowment for Financial Education (NEFE); Tom Bradley, TD Ameritrade; Joel Bruckenstein, Virtual Office News; Kurt Cerulli, Cerulli Associates; David Hunt, McKinsey & Co.; Deena Katz and Dr. William Gustafson, Texas Tech University, Division of Personal Financial Planning; Jay Lanigan, former Fidelity Investments executive; Feng Liu, Financial Planning Standard Council of China (FPSCC); Noel Maye, Financial Planning Standards Board (FPSB); Don Phillips, Morningstar; Peter Sundman, Neuberger Berman, LLC; Mark Tibergien, Moss Adams, LLC; David Tittsworth, Investment Adviser Association (IAA); Donald B. Trone, Foundation for Fiduciary Studies; Marvin W. Tuttle, Jr. and Duane Thompson, Financial Planning Association (FPA); and Tom Winnick, DWS Scudder.

We also wish to thank the industry associations and educational institutions that are an important part of this community and were invaluable resources to us: College for Financial Planning, National Endowment for Financial Education (NEFE), Investment Management Consultants Association (IMCA), Certified Financial Planning Board of Standards, Inc. (CFP Board), Financial Planning Association (FPA), Financial Planning Standards Board (FPSB), National Association of Personal Financial Advisors (NAPFA), and the Investment Adviser Association (IAA).

We are grateful to Dr. Saul Feldman, chairman emeritus of United Behavioral Health in San Francisco, and Craig Fiebig of Seattle, who freely shared their perspectives and experiences as clients of independent investment advisers.

Heartfelt thanks to our writer, Robert Casey, who had the challenging task of researching and assembling a vast amount of industry history and information into this remarkable story; to our extraordinary editor Nancy Friedman, whose talent with words helped shape the narrative into its final form; and to Ann Simon of Schwab Institutional and our project manager Nancy Chandler, who together shepherded the book's development. We are indebted to Randall Goodall and the team at Seventeenth Street Studios and to our copy editor, Karen Seriguchi.

For their generous assistance, industry perspective, background materials, and resources, we would like to thank our Schwab colleagues.

We owe a debt of thanks to our Schwab book review committee, who took on the burden of this assignment in addition to their normal responsibilities. David Canter, Joanne Cuthbertson, Greg Gable, Pam Lewis, Angie Popek, and David Welling were invaluable in guiding the manuscript's development.

We also thank the former Schwab executives who shared their memories, time, and expertise. John Philip Coghlan, former president of Schwab Institutional; Jim Hackley, former senior vice president and general manager of Schwab Institutional; John McGonigle, former senior vice president, office of the chairman and chief executive officer, Charles Schwab & Co., Inc.; Dan Leemon, former executive vice president and chief strategy officer of Charles Schwab & Co., Inc.; and Joshua Rymer, former senior vice president and head of Schwab Institutional strategy.

We also want to thank other Schwab colleagues who have been resources as we developed the book. They include Jon Beatty, Doug Beck, Hilary Bernstein, Jeff Brown, Lucy Carrico, Ron Carter, Bernie Clark, Ed Cooper, David DeVoe, Leslie Eggerling, Anita Fox, Rob Gegenwarth, Gage Gilham, Gerry Groninger, Barnaby Grist, Doug Hanson, Edie Heilman, Steve Hirsch, David Hutchinson, Scot Kobashigawa, Mike Kurtz, Philip Lee, Natalie Lera, Brad Losson, Katrina Lundstedt, Glen Mathison, Tim Oden, Rich Policastro, Mark Port, Tina Ritko, Scot Rister, Myra Rothfeld, Dan Skiles, Bill Thomas, Alison Wertheim, and Lisa Wright.

Special thanks go to Tim Kochis, Noel Maye, and Dan Leemon, who reviewed the manuscript and provided encouragement, editorial suggestions, constructive criticism, and invaluable insights as well as introductions to important resources and people. Their extraordinary support helped make this book possible.

Last but certainly not least, our thanks to all the employees of Schwab Institutional, past and present, for their unwavering dedication and commitment to helping advisers grow, compete, and succeed over the past decades and into the future.

ONE

Investing with a Difference

THEY CALLED IT a new paradigm for business, built on "network effects" and "mind share."

"Not since Bill Gates took Microsoft public in 1986 has Wall Street witnessed anything like the wealth-creating power of today's Internet stocks," wrote a *Time* magazine reporter in June 1998. "Internet or Bust," proclaimed the cover of *Fortune* magazine in December of that year. "Every category is being inundated," an analyst told the *New York Times* in September 1999. "No one wants to miss the boat."

There were tales of fledgling companies spending $30,000, $50,000, even $250,000 on self-congratulatory parties. Of day traders making fortunes in minutes with a few clicks on a keyboard. Of traditional industries—natural gas, groceries, toys—being transformed by information technology.

In the late 1990s, investors by the thousands were caught up in a soaring, exhilarating ride. As the new century dawned—and fears of a "Y2K" technology disaster turned out to be baseless—the markets continued to inch their way upward. The Dow Jones peaked at 11,722.98 on January 14, 2000, the technology-heavy NASDAQ Composite hit an all-time high of 5,048.62 on March 10, and the broader Standard & Poor's 500 index reached 1,553.11 on March 24. Many

1

Investors watch helplessly
as the technology-laden
NASDAQ continues its
downward slide

entrepreneurs and investors reveled in their sudden wealth: one dollar invested in the S&P 500 in 1995 had grown to $3.50 by January 2000.[1] Investors who had focused on technology stocks often did even better: some boasted of eightfold or greater gains. The media were swept up in the excitement. Some market-watchers foresaw "a long boom"[2] or predicted that the Dow would eventually reach 36,000.[3]

And then, just as the days were lengthening into spring, the ride stopped short.

The U.S. stock market's reversal didn't come as a sickening one-day plunge like Black Friday in 1929, which signaled the beginning of the Great Depression, or like the 508-point fall in the Dow on October 19, 1987, the largest one-day market drop in history. But this skidding decline, which took 18 months to hit bottom, was a shocking wake-up call nonetheless. By late September 2002, when the NASDAQ closed at 1,185, the bear market had resulted in the loss of $4.4 trillion in market value. It was the largest stock market collapse in the history of industrial capitalism.[4]

Yet when the dust settled, one group of investors found itself in surprisingly good financial shape. Throughout the bull market, these investors' portfolios had been diversified, asset allocated, and lacking the riskier "new paradigm" holdings. Now, as dot-com businesses were going bankrupt and stock values dwindling to near zero, this group of investors found themselves relatively unscathed and marveling at their good fortune.

But it wasn't luck that had led to their survival. Rather, it was foresight, prudence, and invaluable professional assistance. Diverse as they were—families planning for retirement, businesspeople charting a course for success, institutions seeking financial guidance—these investors had one important factor in common: they were clients of independent registered investment advisers.

a breed apart

Throughout the bull market of the 1990s, many independent advisers had been skeptical about dot-com enterprises that seemed built on nothing but promises. They'd spoken up for balance and moderation—even when their clients urged them to jump on the dot-com bandwagon. But independent advisers maintained their independence and persisted in focusing not on the sale of investment products to a client but on their clients' investment goals.

For independent advisers, there was nothing radical about this approach. It was the same strategy they had been taking since "investment counselors" first emerged as a profession during another fabled bull market: the reckless 1920s. Then, too, many independent advisers counseled prudence and balance. Then, too, some advisers' clients felt envious of their "luckier" counterparts—and were vindicated when they weathered the crash and the Depression with relatively lighter losses.

Why was this so? Where did independent advisers get their independence? How did the profession emerge, develop, and thrive? What challenges did it face on its path to growth? What makes independent adviser firms different—and successful?

First, though, a more basic question: what are independent advisers, and what do they do?

Perhaps it's easiest to answer that question by saying what they are not and what they don't do. Independent advisers generally don't sell specific products; rather, many emphasize a personalized financial plan and investment strategy as a means of controlling their

"The typical client of an independent registered investment adviser appreciates that the adviser is an advocate for the client—not for a particular solution."

—MARK TIBERGIEN,
MOSS ADAMS, LLP

clients' financial risk. Rather than depend on sales commissions, as traditional brokers do, they generally charge a defined fee, and their fee structure is fully disclosed to clients. Fee-based independent advisers sell advice, pure and simple. (Although, to be sure, advice about the financial markets is rarely a simple matter.) In short, they make more when their clients' assets increase.

They also are entrepreneurs with the natural eagerness of small-business owners to satisfy their customers and the nimbleness to innovate quickly.

For decades, many independent advisers have arrived at the profession from financial planning, which values idealism, strict ethical standards, and strategies to assist clients in meeting financial and life goals. To compete with major financial institutions, many of them have obtained professional credentials such as the Certified Financial Planner certification and Chartered Financial Analyst. They've shown they are eager to learn and share insights from the academic world.

These elements add up to a client-driven service model distinctly different from the product-driven service model that has traditionally dominated the financial services industry. Clients perceive the distinction, says Mark Tibergien, a principal with Moss Adams, an accounting and consulting firm to the adviser industry. "It's the difference between whether advice or product is the leading-edge offering," Tibergien said. "The typical client of an independent registered investment adviser appreciates that the adviser is an advocate for the client—not for a particular solution."

Don Phillips, a managing director at the mutual fund data service Morningstar, who joined that firm in 1986 as its first mutual fund analyst, agrees. "Independent advisers have flourished because they put the investor's interest first," he said. "That's been the mission of many of the people who choose to go the independent route. They genuinely want to do what's right for their clients. I take great joy in seeing our clients succeed in the marketplace, because it shows that the investment world is ultimately a meritocracy. People who do the right thing win in the long run."

Studies show that consumers give higher ratings to independent advisers—on both objectivity and skill—than to advisers at large

Financial services firms have a credibility gap with consumers on retirement

 : What is your overall impression of the ability of the following institutions to address your household's needs for retirement-related products and advice?

	Independent financial advisors	Top 3 investment companies	Top 5 brokerage firms	Top 5 life insurers	Top 5 banks
Positive	43%	40%	28%	24%	18%
Neutral	10%	5%	16%	9%	8%
Negative	47%	55%	56%	67%	74%

SOURCE: McKinsey & Co., *Affluent Consumer Survey*, 2004; team analysis

Consumers' perceptions of financial firms on their retirement capabilities

Q: How would you describe the ability of the following institutions to address your retirement needs?

	Percent perceiving as "able" in 2006	PTT change in perceived "ability" since 2004
Independent financial advisors	69	+ 4%
Top three investment companies	67	- 17
Top five brokerage firms	61	- 21
Top five banks	57	+ 4
Top five life insurers	48	- 12

SOURCE: McKinsey & Co., *2006 Consumer Retirement Survey*

financial institutions. A recent research report on retirement issues by management consulting firm McKinsey & Company found a widespread belief among consumers that most financial advisers are primarily interested in "pushing products" rather than providing unbiased advice. The report also said fewer than one-third of survey respondents "received even the most rudimentary forms of retirement advice from their financial providers." There was one notable exception to this disappointing picture, the report said: the independent adviser segment. "Here retirees and pre-retirees alike claimed to be receiving a significantly higher level of retirement advice than consumers utilizing any other segment. At the same time, independent financial advisers scored the highest marks along such key customer satisfaction dimensions as product knowledge and overall advice capabilities."[5]

There's a good reason independent advisers get better ratings, says David Hunt, director of the McKinsey study: they do a better job. Americans are coming up against serious risks, and "in the face of those retirement risks, you can see independent financial planners stepping forward." He continued:

> What our research shows, and what other people have also observed and written about, is that independent advisers were among the first to understand these demographic trends. They were among the first to put together teams of people who could handle retirement advice. They are more likely to talk with their clients about retirement. They are more likely to raise these sensitive issues than either investment firms or brokerage firms. They're more likely to have a referral network of people who can talk about health care or trusts or insurance as well as investments, so that the client is getting a holistic package. They have an entrepreneurial spirit, so there's a real drive that you find in small businesses of all kinds for client service. And they have a pricing mechanism that has given them the ability to be seen by their clients—we can argue whether this is truth or perception—as being more independent.
>
> And they are the fastest-growing segment. We believe that over the last couple of years they have continued to put a distance between themselves and the brokerage and investment management firms.

learning and innovating

To stay ahead, independent advisers have had to be good advocates for their clients. They've had to be willing to learn, to try new techniques, and to share their ideas with peers. They've also been able to adopt new practices quickly.

Independent advisers in general tend to favor lower-cost investment vehicles when appropriate for their clients. For example, independent advisers were early and important champions of both index funds and exchange-traded funds, two low-cost passive investment vehicles. They encouraged Morningstar to develop an investment style grid, which became its now-famous mutual fund Style Box, and then pioneered its use as a tool both to analyze funds and to explain complex investment concepts.

New ideas spread quickly among independent advisers because they are active networkers and enthusiastic participants in industry associations that encourage ongoing education. The Financial Planning Association, which has more than a hundred local chapters, sponsors study groups—a common feature in the legal, medical, and accounting professions, but rare among large financial institutions. So does the National Association of Personal Financial Advisors, whose members are fee-only advisers. Study groups usually meet monthly or quarterly to analyze hypothetical case studies, an exercise that sharpens advisers' skills. Group discussions encourage the sharing of best practices and insights and allows participants to benefit from their colleagues' expertise. Sometimes a guest speaker will talk about specific financial planning topics, investments, or practice management issues such as technology or regulatory compliance. A few study groups are regional or even national in scope; some, such as

> Advisers encouraged Morningstar to develop an investment style grid, which became its now-famous Morningstar Style Box™, introduced in 1992

the Alpha Group and the Capstone Group, have evolved into prestigious, invitation-only organizations with limited membership.

"I'm amazed by how open financial advisers are to learning about different topics," Morningstar's Phillips said. "Not just the legal information you need to know for estate planning, or the mathematics of investing, but also the psychology of working with clients. And none of it with the short-term, let's-close-the-sale mentality. It's done with a view toward creating a better experience for the investor."

Not only do independent advisers constitute a community of learners, Phillips added, "but it's a community full of people who are eager to share what they've learned with their peers."

focused on the client

Gary Furukawa, the president and chief investment officer of Freestone Capital Management, an independent investment advisory firm in Seattle, Washington, is an accountant by training. But what he likes best about his job isn't the numbers. His favorite challenge and biggest enjoyment, he said, lie in helping clients understand—and realize—their goals:

> It's a puzzle I like figuring out. Often clients will tell you one thing but mean something else. It's fun to figure out their true objectives. And then it's really fun to figure out how you're going to get them there.

> People don't spend their days thinking about this stuff. So when you first meet with someone, there's a process of uncovering the real issues. We always say that part of our role is to be a psychiatrist. And that part is very interesting to me—to get to the bottom of it and figure out what's really important to them.

One of the most challenging areas, even for advisers who've been trained as counselors, is investment risk. Gauging the desirable risk level of an investment portfolio involves understanding the client's time horizon—how soon the assets must be available for spending. The longer the horizon, the riskier a portfolio can afford to be. A second factor is the client's capacity for risk. Substantial assets may provide a cushion against a loss. But that cushion is meaningless if the client has a low tolerance for risk. And that factor is the most difficult to quantify: With how much risk is the client emotionally comfortable? To answer the question, some advisers administer questionnaires (although many experts and practitioners are skeptical of their validity or practicality). Others use questionnaires simply as the basis for discussion, a practice known as risk coaching.

One successful advocate of risk coaching is Evensky and Katz, an independent advisory firm based in Coral Gables, Florida. The firm's thirteen-page risk tolerance questionnaire focuses clients on investment goals and time horizons. It also helps them understand the trade-off involved between return and risk.

"It's simply a framework for us and the client to have a meaningful discussion about risk," said Deena Katz, principal and former president of the firm. "It's not useful to ask a client to rate on a scale of one to a hundred how much investment in equities he or she would feel comfortable with. How do they know? And their comfort level changes. If the market's going up, they may have zero concern about risk. And if the market's going down, they may have zero tolerance for risk."

Because risk tolerance will vary over time, Evensky and Katz sees risk coaching as an ongoing part of its job, not just a topic to discuss with new clients. "We take all our clients through risk coaching, though some need coaching much more often than others," Katz said. "We'll have that discussion once a year or when there is a big change in the market. We go back and ask some key questions to see if everybody is still singing from the same hymn book."

Many independent advisers offer more than counseling and advice. Indeed, they are client advocates. For example, independent advisers have pressed the mutual fund industry to make many changes to benefit investors. One such change was fund naming. "The labeling of funds used to be sloppy," Morningstar's Phillips said. "Janus, Windsor, Magellan—they're nice names, but they don't tell you anything about how the fund is going to be managed. Advisers demanded a higher level of precision. They wanted more institutional quality and they wanted more truth in labeling." With encouragement eventually from the U.S. Securities and Exchange Commission, the industry began more consistently to use names—

Independent advisers are as diverse as the clients they serve. Some manage hundreds of billions of dollars in assets for institutions such as mutual funds, pension plans, or endowments. Others are hedge fund managers who serve both institutional and individual clients.

The largest category comprises advisers whose clients are mostly individuals. Their firms generally are small—two employees to a few dozen—and are not owned by or affiliated with larger organizations. Their annual revenue ranges between $1 million and $10 million. Most are local businesses with a strong connection to their community. That connection is often most apparent in times of crisis:

For example, after 9/11 and Hurricane Katrina, independent advisers (a number of whom were themselves affected by the catastrophes) responded quickly and generously.

Most are local businesses with a strong connection to their local community.

Independent advisory firms fall into four general practice types, according to Cerulli Associates, a leading financial industry research firm.[6]

WEALTH MANAGERS oversee 53 percent of the investment assets managed by independents. They provide comprehensive planning and asset-management services, primarily to high-net-worth individuals.

MONEY MANAGERS represent 27 percent of assets. Their clients are predominantly individuals, but they also serve small institutions such as retirement plans and endowments.

FINANCIAL PLANNERS manage 12 percent of investment assets. They provide comprehensive planning, but don't necessarily oversee investments or otherwise implement the plans they create.

INVESTMENT PLANNERS, a relatively new hybrid type, control 8 percent of assets. They combine money management services and planning and investment advice.

According to the Cerulli report, the once-distinct line between institutional advisers (such as pension fund managers) and advisers catering to individuals has blurred. As defined-benefit plans have dwindled, and their asset growth slowed, some institutional managers have turned to individual clients for new business. And firms that once served only individuals now find they can attract institutional business as well.

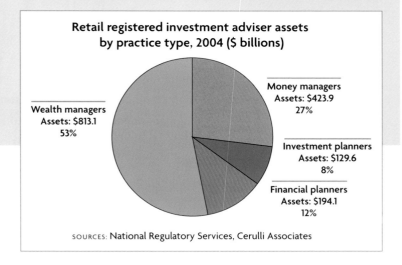

Retail registered investment adviser assets by practice type, 2004 ($ billions)

Wealth managers
Assets: $813.1
53%

Money managers
Assets: $423.9
27%

Investment planners
Assets: $129.6
8%

Financial planners
Assets: $194.1
12%

SOURCES: National Regulatory Services, Cerulli Associates

growth, value, and so on—reflective of the funds' investment objectives.

In the early 1990s, as client counseling was growing in importance, independent advisers began to investigate a new field of study, behavioral finance. As its name suggests, behavioral finance is a marriage of psychology and economics, and it takes a skeptical view toward both disciplines. It questions the concept of efficient markets that underpins much of modern finance. And it asks whether individual investors act rationally to maximize their returns.

Innovators by definition, many independent advisers became ardent students of the new discipline. Prominent researchers, such as psychologist Daniel Kahneman of Princeton University and behavioral-finance theorist Richard Thaler of the University of Chicago, began to speak at meetings of independent advisers. Their studies showed how people can be hobbled by emotions, cognitive shortcuts, and mental mistakes where money is concerned. A frequent research topic of behaviorists was regret. Their studies found that people make decisions with an eye toward avoiding regret down the road, a course of action that may cause them to act against their best interests. For example, investors tend to hold on to stocks that have lost money while selling winners. Why? Until the loss is realized, they can avoid facing the pain of regret caused by a failed investment.

Except for the pocket of enthusiastic support among independent advisers, behavioral finance remained an academic discipline generally ignored by Wall Street and the rest of the investment community. Then, in 2002, Kahneman was awarded the Nobel Prize in economics—despite his being a psychologist, not an economist. The award confirmed the significance of behavioral finance research and confirmed what independent advisers had discovered years earlier: behavioral finance helps them do a better job for their clients.

a force to be reckoned with

Long before *behavioral finance*, *asset allocation*, and *risk tolerance* entered the lexicon, independent advisers were already focused on "doing a better job for clients." As a result, the profession has evolved from a niche service catering to a small group of wealthy Americans

Daniel Kahneman celebrates his 2002 Nobel Prize, which integrated insights from psychological research into economic science

to one of the fastest-growing and most influential segments of the financial services industry. Independent investment advisers and their client-centered approach have already transformed the world of financial services. Now one capability of independent advisers—financial planning—is expanding outside U.S. borders and becoming an important global force.

It's been a remarkable trajectory from the profession's modest yet ambitious beginnings just after World War I, when a few pioneering firms on the East and West coasts separately yet almost simultaneously began focusing on financial counseling, analysis, and planning rather than the traditional emphasis of investment firms: product sales. Over decades of slow growth, Congressional investigations, regulatory challenges, and internal development, the profession gradually solidified and strengthened. The 1974 passage of the Employee Retirement Income Security Act, the growing importance of mutual funds, and the 1975 abolition of fixed brokerage fees set the stage for watershed growth and innovation between the 1980s and early 2000s. Beginning in 1987, brokerage firm Charles Schwab embarked on a pioneering association with independent advisers and their clients, offering them custody and back-office services that helped independent firms thrive. New mutual

THE FIDUCIARY ROLE

Every registered independent investment adviser acts as a *fiduciary,* a term that implies specific rules and legal duties. As fiduciaries, advisers must put their clients' interests first under all circumstances. They also have a duty to act conscientiously on the client's behalf.

Other fiduciary obligations of advisers have emerged from court decisions and SEC regulatory rulings. Advisers are required to

- have a reasonable basis for the investment advice provided to clients;

- offer investment recommendations free of outside influence or undisclosed conflicts;

- render advice suitable to clients' needs, objectives, and financial considerations;

- seek to obtain from brokers the best exection (including price and other terms) for the clients' securities transactions directed by the adviser;

- make a full and fair disclosure to clients of all material facts, particularly regarding potential conflicts of interest.

Every independent registered investment adviser is held to a fiduciary standard based on interpretations of the Investment Advisers Act of 1940. The emphasis is on the process, not the investment outcome. According to the Foundation for Fiduciary Studies, "Even the most aggressive and unconventional asset can meet the standard if arrived at through a sound process, while the most conservative and traditional one may not measure up if a sound process is lacking."[7]

> As fiduciaries, advisers must put their clients' interests first under all circumstances.

Registered investment advisers are also governed by rigorous rules that include disclosures about the firm's business practices, including total assets under management, biographies of key investment personnel, the firm's disciplinary history, and description of the firm's code of ethics. "Disclosures required of advisers registering with the SEC alone are without precedent in other regulated professions," said David G. Tittsworth, executive director of the trade group Investment Adviser Association. "Requiring other professions to disclose their fees—in and of itself— would generate major lobbying efforts to keep the heavy hand of government from bringing down the American system of capitalism."

Form ADV, a two-part document advisers must update annually and make available to clients

fund supermarkets enabled independent advisers to select funds from among many no-load families, with centralized recordkeeping and consolidated client statements. And the technology boom of the 1990s—and the downturn of the early 2000s, exacerbated by the September 11, 2001, disasters—created unprecedented demand for independent financial advice.

Today, the number of affluent investors with complex and sophisticated requirements continues to grow, particularly as millions of members of the baby boom generation approach retirement age. Meeting these opportunities and challenges are a growing number of independent advisers, joined by those in the new category of "advisers turning independent," who are contributing significantly to the growth. Although managing growth—and competition—poses its own demands, independent advisers have never been better positioned to succeed in the United States and around the world.

How did they arrive at this promising juncture? To answer that question, we need to go back nearly a century to the very beginnings of the independent investment advisory industry, when a few individuals, dissatisfied with the status quo, decided they could create something different—and better.

In 1987, Schwab embarked on a pioneering effort to serve the needs of independent advisers

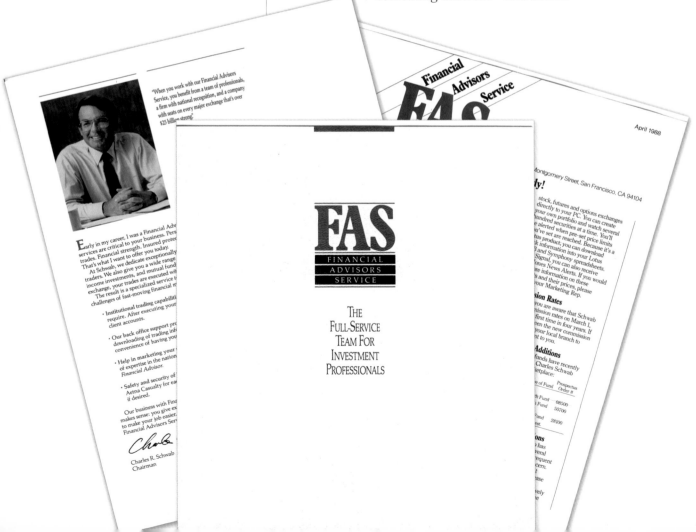

FAS
FINANCIAL
ADVISORS
SERVICE

THE
FULL-SERVICE
TEAM FOR
INVESTMENT
PROFESSIONALS

April 1988

TWO

Birth
of a
Profession

HE INDEPENDENT ADVISER PROFESSION—or "investment
counseling," as it was originally called—owes its existence to
a convergence of events and influences in the first quarter of
the twentieth century. It was shaped by a few tireless, visionary
individuals who saw beyond traditional investment services to a
new model that valued the client relationship more than the financial product. And it was tested and strengthened by a series of
investigations and reforms that grew out of President Franklin D.
Roosevelt's New Deal.

Some background is useful here. In the early years of the twentieth century, corporate America was barely emerging from the era of
the robber barons—bankers and industrialists whose great achievements were often matched by equally great abuses of power. As late
as the 1920s, investing in most American companies was viewed as
a highly risky activity. Pioneering investment adviser Theodore T.
Scudder wrote that "prior to 1900 corporate morals were so low that
common stocks of practically all publicly held companies could be
considered nothing more than outright speculations."[1]

Investment bankers, insurance companies, and professional
trustees dominated the investment profession; none allowed individual investors much control over their investments other than to

say yes or no to a recommendation. The firms that offered investment advice were the same firms that sold investment products.

In 1912, Arsène Pujo, a Democratic congressman from Louisiana, received authorization to form a House committee to investigate the "money trust"—a group of financial leaders who were abusing the public trust to consolidate their control over many industries. The committee's findings lent support to a number of reforms, including the Sixteenth Amendment to the Constitution, which authorized a national income tax and was ratified in 1913; the Federal Reserve Act, also in 1913; and the Clayton Antitrust Act in 1914. The imposition of the federal income tax in particular stimulated interest in investment counsel.

Then came World War I and a second major influence on investment patterns: the issuance of huge numbers of bonds to finance the war effort. The liberty loans, as they were known, were the largest bond issues of their time; by 1919 more than $21 billion in bonds were sold, in denominations of $100 each. Ordinary Americans who had never been "speculators" responded to the U.S. Treasury's exhortations to buy them—some out of patriotism and others because the bond issues were a tax-exempt hedge against the rampant inflation of the war years. In 1917, when the first war bonds were issued, Wall Street investment bankers had estimated that no more than three hundred fifty thousand people would buy them. By 1919 more than eleven million Americans had invested in liberty loans. "Inadvertently," writes Wall Street historian Charles R. Geisst, "the war effort had given the vast majority of small investors a taste for securities that would only grow stronger in the 1920s."[2] Charles Mitchell, president and chairman of the National City Bank (later Citicorp) referred to "a large, new army of investors . . . who may in the future be developed into savers and bond buyers."[3]

A brief, severe recession followed the 1919 Armistice. But by 1922 the United States had made a striking recovery. The country

The 16th Amendment established Congress's right to impose a Federal income tax. In 1913, due to generous exemptions and deductions, less than 1 percent of the population paid income taxes

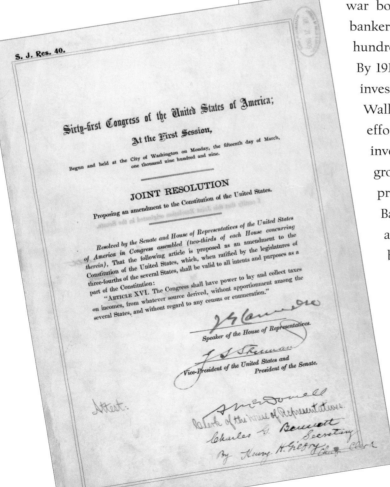

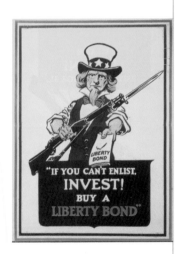

experienced a surge in business activity that raised living standards, generated entrepreneurial wealth, and opened the door to a deluge of securities issuance on Wall Street. Between 1919 and 1929, the annual rate of corporate securities issuance nearly quadrupled. The flood of securities coming to market in those boom years overwhelmed amateur investors. They needed expert help to identify investments with good prospects amid the mass of new issues. As one investment adviser later described the situation, "The average private security buyer, whether he was retired or in active business, or even if he were to some extent connected to finance, had not the time or the money to cover the entire investment field and choose from the securities that were soundest and best suited to his particular objective. And in most cases he did not have the experience."[4] Moreover, the boom was playing out against a backdrop of economic uneasiness. The Federal Reserve was relatively new, and price stability was not yet on the horizon. Between 1913 and 1920, inflation had eroded fully half the dollar's value. Caution, even fear, was the watchword of many investors in the 1920s. Preserving capital and its purchasing power was a major objective.

It was in this environment that a small number of independent advisers—then self-styled as "counselors"—got their start. In general, their clients weren't speculators trying to cash in on a stock tip overheard at a speakeasy. Instead, they tended to be business

THEODORE SCUDDER, FOUNDER, SCUDDER, STEVENS & CLARK

As a young bond salesman in Boston, Theodore Townsend Scudder longed to expand his horizons. Born in 1889, Scudder had graduated from Harvard and gone to work as an office boy at an investment banking firm, then quit because he wasn't being trained for advancement. He returned to the firm in 1912 to take a sales position, at which he excelled. Yet he still wasn't satisfied. "It did not take me more than three months," he later wrote, "to come to the conclusion that although I was selling securities in exactly the same way as other salesmen, I was not doing a good business."

What was missing? A clue came during a conversation Scudder had with Frederic H. Curtiss, chairman of the Federal Reserve Bank of Boston, during a sales call. "Have you looked all over these bonds, and do you think they are perfectly good?" Curtiss later recounted. Yes, he had, Scudder replied. "And then I said, 'Well, how do you know that is what I need?' . . . Well, [Scudder] hesitated and said of course he didn't. . . . Then

> **It became clear that their advice was at least as valuable as their banking services.**

[Scudder] said, 'What is needed here is a separate agency that will give advice and that would have no interest in the things they have to sell.'"

As a result of insights like this one, Scudder left the investment banking firm in 1914 and went into business in Boston under the wing of a local brokerage house. In 1919, he established his own firm, Scudder, Stevens & Clark, with two fellow Harvard alumni, Sidney Stevens and F. Haven Clark.

At first, the three men remained in investment banking, offering investment counsel without charge. But it soon became clear that their advice was at least as valuable as their banking services. So Scudder approached about twenty clients and offered them counsel "on an impartial and increasingly expert basis. We agreed that they would tell us their complete portfolio and other pertinent facts, such as how much life insurance they carried, how much real estate mortgages they owned, what they needed per annum to live on, etc. We would

then diagnose their situation and suggest to them what we believed to be a sound investment program to follow." In return, clients would pay the firm a fee of 1 percent of the value of any securities bought or sold on the firm's advice.

It was a "whole new revolutionary concept where instead of selling products, you're selling advice," observes David G. Tittsworth, executive director of the Investment Adviser Association (IAA) in Washington, D.C. "To me, that's the beginning of the investment adviser business."

Stevens found the concept too radical: After just one year, he retired from an active role in the firm. A few months later, Scudder and Clark wrote a five-page business prospectus in which they established the profession's first principles: offer "unbiased expert advice," create a diversified portfolio, and provide constant supervision of the account.

Scudder died in 1953, before the true flowering of the independent investment adviser profession. But his vision continues to guide every practitioner.

owners, corporate executives, and members of the professions—knowledgeable individuals of means looking for ongoing advice in a challenging investment environment. Rising prosperity had given them the assets to meet the minimum account size required by independent advisers, typically $1 million or more in today's dollars. And waves of innovation, which had brought forth the radio, the refrigerator, and air mail, among other novelties, increased their tolerance for new ideas and made them willing—even eager—to take a chance on independent financial advisory firms. The two new breeds—the independent adviser and the affluent client willing to delegate investment management to a trusted professional—emerged together. Both prospered as a burgeoning economy and a bull market created unprecedented new wealth. Though small in overall numbers—the SEC in 1942 reported just 753 registered advisers[5]—independent advisers represented a significant change in the status quo and an influence much greater than their size would suggest.

the pioneers

Who were the early investment advisers? What inspired them to pioneer a new profession?

Arthur M. Clifford was motivated by chance and imagination. He had opened his brokerage firm in Los Angeles in 1911, when that city's population numbered less than four hundred thousand. In 1915, one of his wealthy clients asked him to review her $30 million in assets, and from then on Clifford called himself an "investment counselor and financial analyst." By 1921, Clifford was focusing exclusively on investment counsel and charging fixed fees for his services. His firm, Clifford Associates, is still active in Pasadena, California.[6]

Across the country in Boston, frustration and restlessness spurred Theodore T. Scudder to invent his own brand of investment counsel. In 1919, the young bond salesman had founded an investment bank with two partners, Sidney Stevens and F. Haven Clark, but he became dissatisfied with the conflicts of interest he faced serving customers of securities firms. Those firms held stocks and bonds from corporate underwritings or their trading inventories and—not coincidentally—often recommended those very securities to their retail customers. The savvier customers protested. Scudder later told the story about one hard-nosed customer to whom he'd tried to sell some bonds. "How do you know I should buy this bond?" the man shot back. "Perhaps I already own too many bonds. Perhaps I should buy more. How can a doctor or lawyer advise you what to do if they don't know all about you?" Finally, before shooing Scudder out of his office, the man declared, "I'd be willing to pay for unbiased advice if I could find it." He became Scudder, Stevens & Clark's first client when the firm left the investment banking business in 1921 to focus solely on investment advice.[7]

Slowly but persistently, other firms followed the lead of the pioneers on both coasts. By 1929 there were as many as seventy "investment counsel" firms throughout the country,[8] including Laurence Booth & Company in Los Angeles; Farwell & Company (later Sheridan, Farwell and Morrison) in Chicago; Cambridge Associates and Eaton & Howard in Boston; Haydock, Cressler & Lamson in Cincinnati; and Investors Economic Services in Milwaukee. In addition to supervising wealthy clients' personal funds, the firms managed their clients' trusts, endowments, and charitable funds. Thus they were not only the country's first independent financial advisers but also the first independent money managers.

The new independent financial advisers differed in striking ways from their predecessors and competitors. First, they focused on their clients' unique needs rather than on selling a particular product. Second, they styled themselves as professional practitioners, emulating lawyers and accountants in the way they dealt with clients. To reduce conflicts of interest, many offered no services other than investment advice. Typically, they helped clients identify investment goals, set priorities, and prepare a formal investment plan. Investments were continuously monitored and supervised. Their fees, usually based on assets under management, were fully disclosed and paid directly by the clients. This method of charging fees required advisers to value client portfolios regularly and helped direct the attention of investment professionals to the performance of the client's total holdings. The experience of Scudder, Stevens & Clark illustrates the evolution of fee arrangements. When it entered the business, the firm charged 1 percent of all transaction amounts, either sales or purchases, with brokerage charges coming

To reduce conflicts of interest, many advisers offered no services other than investment advice.

out of Scudder's fee. Not only did that approach generate inadequate revenue, it also—contrary to the firm's philosophy—encouraged transactions. Scudder replaced that structure with a one-half percent fee on assets, with the brokerage fee being paid by the clients, and soon imposed a 1 percent fee on assets with breakpoints for larger account balances.[9]

A third innovation was financial planning. As a discipline and a profession, financial planning would not be recognized until the early 1970s (the College for Financial Planning, founded in Denver in 1972, was the nation's first financial planning educational institution). But these early independent advisers pioneered some of the essential tools of the financial planning process. In his 1940 testimony to the Senate Banking Committee, Charles M. O'Hearn of Clarke, Sinsabaugh & Co. in New York described his firm's approach in a way most modern financial planners would recognize and endorse:

> Our first task is to prepare and maintain for each client a broad plan for his general financial objectives and for the methods appropriate to their accomplishment. . . . In making the plan, we must determine the soundness of the relation of his income to his standard of living. We must also consider his capacity to assume financial risks, his probable future expenses for educating his family, the number of his dependents, and so forth. We must establish with each client a relationship of trust and confidence designed to last over a long period of time because economic forces work themselves out slowly. Business and investment cycles last for years and our investment plans have to be similarly long-range. . . . It is not our objective to make money for him in a series of spectacular moves.[10]

Above all, independent advisers believed that ethical standards, professional objectivity, and trust were the keys to their success. When the Investment Counsel Association of America (predecessor to the Investment Adviser Association), the industry's first trade group, adopted its code of professional practice in 1937, an important provision was that "neither the firm nor any partner, executive or employee thereof should directly or indirectly engage in any activity which may jeopardize the firm's ability to render unbiased investment advice."[11]

bright spots in the depression

The 1929 stock market crash and the decade-long Great Depression that followed brought misery to millions of Americans. In contrast, independent advisers fared relatively well as a group and even managed to expand their business. Because they charged fees based on assets under management and tended to follow conservative investing strategies—with a focus on investment-grade fixed-income securities—independent advisers could keep their clients, and themselves, afloat. Treasury bonds, for example, were a mainstay of conservative investors. One dollar invested in U.S. Treasury bonds at the start of 1930 was worth $1.27 five years later. By contrast, a dollar invested in the stock market shrank to 59 cents over the same period. Then, as now, asset allocation made all the difference in investing, and asset allocation—not yet called by that name, but known rather as "don't put all your eggs in one basket"—was what independent advisers specialized in. Whatever pain they suffered from the stock market crash, independent advisers' clients benefited because their money was being professionally managed.

Investors stunned by the 1929 stock market crash gather at the Sub-Treasury building on Wall Street

"Hoovervilles" for the homeless appeared across the United States during the Great Depression

Unemployed workers turned to selling apples to avoid the shame of panhandling

However, that did not minimize the overall bleakness of the economic landscape. The shrinking economy left one in four workers jobless in 1933.[12] Between 1930 and 1932, industrial stocks lost 80 percent of their value, and even blue-chip stock investors suffered painful losses. President Herbert Hoover struggled unsuccessfully to turn the economy around. In derisive recognition of his failure, camps of homeless people springing up throughout the country became known as Hoovervilles. On Wall Street, business was in shambles and the stock markets thoroughly discredited. The term then used for brokers—"customers' men"—carried a bitter irony, because customers were in scarce supply. Securities firms declared "apple days," when brokers were encouraged to take unpaid leave and supplement their income by selling apples on the streets.

The nation's economic woes were not the consequence of unseen global forces, as some apologists tried to argue. Real people and their misdeeds were at fault. In angry response, reformers wanted new laws to regulate the securities markets and prevent fraud. After Franklin D. Roosevelt's landslide presidential victory in 1932, they got their wish: public investigations and hearings continued throughout the decade and exposed a scandalous record of abuse.

FERDINAND PECORA: CRUSADING INVESTIGATOR

Ferdinand Pecora, a shoemaker's son, ferreted out Wall Street's secrets

Facing him in the dock were some of America's most influential men, whose names were synonymous with power, privilege, and great wealth. But Ferdinand J. Pecora—a shoemaker's son born in Sicily in 1882—proved more than equal to the task of interrogating them. He had earned his stripes as an assistant New York district attorney in the 1920s, when he had successfully prosecuted corrupt politicians and questionable stock salesmen. By the time he was appointed chief counsel to the U.S. Senate Banking Committee, in early 1933, Pecora was ready to come out swinging against the most prominent bankers and brokers in the country.

A brilliant, sarcastic cross-examiner, Pecora personally questioned many of the most prominent witnesses, including Charles Mitchell, president and chairman of the National City Bank (later Citicorp); Samuel Insull, head of a huge utilities empire in Illinois; and J. P. ("Jack") Morgan II, of J. P. Morgan and Company. Pecora elicited that Morgan had paid no personal income tax in 1930, 1931, and 1932, and that his bank, like many others, had used "preferred lists" to extend financial privileges to its best clients. It was painful evidence of the insulation of financial elites at a time when most Americans were scraping to get by. Pecora became a hero of reformers and working people and was featured, cigar clenched between his teeth, on the cover of *Time* magazine. By the end of 1933, Congress had passed two landmark pieces of reform legislation, the Glass-Steagall Act and the Securities Act. More reforms would follow in succeeding years.

When the Pecora hearings concluded in July 1934, President Roosevelt appointed Pecora a commissioner of the new Securities and Exchange Commission; Pecora resigned in 1935 and was appointed a New York State Supreme Court judge. His 1939 book, *Wall Street under Oath: The Story of Our Modern Money Changers,* gave an insider's account of the Pecora Commission hearings. After running unsuccessfully for New York City mayor in 1950, Pecora joined a private law practice. Uncharacteristically, he took on some large companies as clients; in 1954, he successfully represented Warner Bros. Pictures Distributing Corporation—accused of antitrust violations—before the U.S. Supreme Court. Pecora died in 1971.

Admitting he had not paid income taxes, famed banker and financier J. P. Morgan (standing, right), takes his seat before the Senate Banking and Currency Committee

Hearings conducted by Ferdinand Pecora, counsel for the Senate Banking and Currency Committee, built support for reform legislation

First in the dock were the bankers. In hearings before the Senate Banking Committee, which commanded the whole country's attention, chief counsel Ferdinand Pecora, a former New York City prosecutor, avoided economic complexities. Instead, he dragged in top financiers and grilled them relentlessly about Wall Street's misdeeds during the 1920s. Among those eventually exposed was Albert Wiggin, chairman of the Chase National Bank and the bank's largest shareholder; he made several million dollars selling short the shares of his own bank as the stock market tumbled, then laundered the profits through Canada to avoid paying income tax.[13]

For weeks, Pecora put on a mesmerizing show while building a copious record to support fundamental reforms being prepared by the new administration. "The Pecora findings created a tidal wave of anger against Wall Street," financial historian Ron Chernow wrote in 1990. "As people followed the hearings on their farms and in their offices, on soup lines and in Hoovervilles, they became convinced that they'd been conned in the 1920s. Yesterday's gods were no more than greedy little devils. Even most of Wall Street was shocked."[14]

Congress responded with waves of reform legislation. The Glass-Steagall Act of 1933 prohibited most securities activities by commercial banks and addressed abuses uncovered by Pecora; it was part of a comprehensive banking bill that also established federal deposit

President Franklin Delano Roosevelt appointed Joseph P. Kennedy, Sr. (center), to serve as the first chairman of the SEC on June 30, 1934

insurance and ultimately separated banking from brokerage. The Securities Act of 1933 and the Securities Exchange Act of 1934 became the basis of fundamental regulation of the securities industry. A Federal Trade Commission investigation and a new round of congressional hearings focused on the interstate holding companies that had gobbled up utilities in the 1920s; the result was the Public Utility Holding Company Act of 1935, which outlawed interstate utilities holding companies and strengthened utility regulation.

The public may have been shocked by the revelations, but none of the targets of the investigations should have been truly caught off guard. The bankers, for example, knew full well that regulation was on its way before Ferdinand Pecora first appeared in the headlines; after all, Roosevelt had made Wall Street reform a campaign pledge. Abuses had endangered the financial health and shareholder profits of the utilities and investment companies as well. They would not be allowed to recur. And buried in the Public Utility Holding Company Act of 1935, which addressed those abuses, was a passage that would have surprising and lasting effects on a formerly overlooked profession: independent investment advisers.[15]

independent advisers: the next target

For a while, independent advisers seemed immune from legislative scrutiny. But a young SEC lawyer named David Schenker, who had served on Pecora's staff and conducted his own eight-year investigation into investment trusts, soon stepped into his mentor's shoes. While not as ferocious or high-profile as Pecora, Schenker was equally determined and savvy. An easy-to-overlook passage in the Public Utility Holding Company Act of 1935 included a congressional command to the SEC to investigate investment companies, known then as investment trusts and today called mutual funds, which had lent a hand in financing the utility manipulations. The SEC found that some $7 billion worth of investment trusts had been floated at the end of the 1920s; by 1935 their assets were worth just $2 billion. As *Time* magazine put it in August 1936, "It became SEC's job to find out where, how and why the rest disappeared."[16]

Soon after the probe got under way, Schenker decided to take a look at the investment advisers who managed the trusts' portfolios. "It became quite obvious to us that there were a great many of them and we felt duty bound to make that study," Schenker testified. When the agency couldn't come up with the names of advisory firms, it decided it needed legislation to get them to report in on their own. Said Schenker:

> Now, we canvassed every source we could and we learned of the existence of 394 investment counselors. That, in my opinion, does not even approximate the number of people who are engaged in this profession, or business, or type of activity. After all, the only way we could get that list is through the telephone directories. But there are many who do not even have telephones, or have their offices in their hats. We could not obtain any information about them. Therefore our fundamental approach to this problem, before we could intelligently make an appraisal of the economic function or the abuses which might exist in that type of organization, [was] to see if we could get something approximating a compulsory census. Fundamentally, that is the basic approach of [the Investment Advisers Act legislation.].[17]

A July 1937 *New York Herald Tribune* article told of plans for the industry's first trade association

Code Is Planned For Investment Counsel Trade

Impending U. S. Control Spurs Effort to Form a National Organization

By Luttrell Maclin

Investment counselors, representing the largest field directly associated with the securities business not regulated now by the Federal government, are planning to form an association which will be a means of enlightening the public as to their true function, and will afford a measure of self-regulation of a sufficiently high order to protect the profession from governmental criticism.

The first indication that the Securities and Exchange Commission was interested in the relation of this field to the general securities business came some months ago when a meeting of investment counselors was called by an officer of the S. E. C. to discuss with them their relation to the public, and particularly investment trusts.

Since the original gatherings, leaders in the field have held numerous private meetings in an endeavor to formulate a charter and code of principles which could be used as the basis for such an association. The youth of the profession (the first large investment ᵌformed in 1919, and

In the early part of the last century, when the first independent advisers—Theodore T. Scudder, Arthur M. Clifford, and their contemporaries—were setting up shop, no term existed to describe their profession. They settled on *investment counsel,* which comprised education and "unbiased expert advice." *Counselor* remained the preferred term for several decades. The Investment Counsel Association of America, the first nonprofit organization to represent the new profession, was founded in 1937 in response to the Securities and Exchange Commission's moves to investigate investment trusts; the ICAA later played a role in the creation of the Investment Advisers Act of 1940.

The act further defined *counselor* and restricted its use:

only advisers who rendered "investment supervisory service" and gave "continuous advice as to the investment of funds on the basis of the individual needs of each client" could call themselves "investment counselors." The definition intentionally excluded others who were required to register under the 1940 act, such as newsletter publishers who dispensed advice but didn't manage money.

Gradually, however, practitioners began using *adviser* instead of *counselor* as an umbrella term, with *counselor* as a subset. In 1975, the ICAA established the Chartered Investment

Counselor program "to recognize the special qualifications of persons employed by member firms whose primary duties are consistent with section 208(c) of the Investment Advisers Act of 1940 (pertaining to the use of the term 'investment counsel')." The ICAA changed its name in 2005 to The Investment Adviser Association. Most states require licensing for investment adviser representatives through an exam called the Series 65. In addition, to use certain industry trade group marks such as "Certified Financial Planner," "Certified Financial Consultants," "Certified Financial Analysts," and "Certified Investment Counselors," such industry groups require practitioners to pass specific certification exams.

The Investment Counsel Association of America, formed in 1937, became the Investment Adviser Association in 2005

oup Formed
by Investment
Counsel Here

Rose to Head Organization; Officers, Directors and Code of Ethics Approved

Investment Counsel Association of America was formally organized yesterday, and officers, directors and a code of professional ... ere approved at a meeting ... the Bankers Club. Dwight ...se, of Brundage, Story & Rose, ... elected president, to serve until the first annual meeting, to be held in May, 1938.

The rapid growth of the investment counsel profession since the formation of the first firm in 1919 has shown clearly the need of a professional organization, to promote the interests of its practitioners, the organizers maintain. Investment counseling is the largest field directly associated with the securities business that is not now under state or Federal regulation, but it is well known that members of the Securities and Exchange Commission have interested themselves in prospective regulation, particularly Commissioner William O. Douglas and Dr. Paul Gourrich, director of the research division.

The code of professional ethics adopted yesterday attempts to set up in a broad manner the objectives of the association, and at the same time to create stand...

While acknowledging that most advisers wanted to do good work for their clients, Schenker testified, "they are impeded in doing that job by the fact that there is a fringe of people who do not perform this function, but who, if I may use the expression, cash in on the goodwill of the reputable organizations . . . by giving themselves a designation of investment counselors. These individuals are nothing more than tipsters, who have outrageous arrangements with respect to profit sharing, and so on."

It was true that at the time the field was essentially unregulated and inevitably attracted some unscrupulous operators. In the 1930s, only six states specifically regulated investment advisers: California, Connecticut, Michigan, New Hampshire, Oklahoma, and Rhode Island. Tip sheets published by stock touts, who promoted stocks in an effort to boost prices, offered hot picks to subscribers, often in league with profit-seeking speculators. Hustlers posing as advisers used other scams as well to bilk the unsuspecting. Many of these activities could be prosecuted under state and local fraud statutes, but some fell through the legal cracks.

The dilemma faced by Schenker, as well as the profession itself, was how to weed out the bad elements without impairing the business of reputable firms.

Realizing that they were in the spotlight and would likely be subject to new federal regulation, independent advisers began meeting among themselves. Some pushed to organize a trade association to represent their profession; after lengthy arguments the Investment Counsel Association of America was formed in 1937. (The association changed its name to the Investment Adviser Association in April 2005.) Some of the bigger firms, like Scudder, Stevens & Clark, declined to join, even though several of their alumni took leading roles in the new organization. According to an internal Scudder history, "By joining, Scudder would bring prestige to the new organization, which could benefit these [smaller, newer] competitors."[18] ICAA joiners and holdouts were united only by their opposition to Schenker's regulatory scheme. The advisers "as a group were ill-prepared for the legislative and bureaucratic assaults. They knew their hearts were pure, they sold nothing but advice, each was single-mindedly struggling to make it the best advice available anywhere . . . and each new development in the long series came as a shock, much like an insult; how could anyone have the effrontery to raise serious demanding questions about the good-hearted victims of this new inquisition?"[19]

In its report to Congress in 1939, the SEC discussed four problem areas with investment advisers: "tipster" services masquerading as bona fide investment advisory firms; the use of performance fees to compensate advisers; the lack of solvency standards for advisers with custody of client assets; and the practice of assigning adviser agreements to other advisers without client consent. Although the agency never cited any specific instances of abuse in the testimony presented to Congress, it did include a general declaration implying problems among investment advisers in its draft legislation.

Many advisers questioned whether the SEC had even come close to demonstrating the need for legislation covering them. In a letter to the Senate, Augustus P. Loring Jr., an investment adviser and private trustee in Boston, quoted the SEC's own report in which the agency acknowledged its study was not detailed and failed to examine any particular firms. "It would seem that the comprehensive type of regulation of investment counsel contemplated by the bill . . . should not be attempted without detailed study," Loring wrote. "Prior to the enactment of such legislation there should be a presentation of very convincing testimony to the effect that such regulation would prevent repetition of existing abuses, and would be for the public good."[20] Douglas T. Johnston, an adviser with Johnston & Lagerquist of New York, echoed Loring's comments: "Here the cart would seem to be before the horse—a bill is being proposed to include all investment advisers with certain important exceptions, not to correct predetermined abuses, but to discover whether they exist."[21]

The legislation aroused little interest outside the small coterie of investment advisory firms. Exemptions for banks, broker-dealers, lawyers, and accountants assured that those groups were not going to object. Although the number of individuals offering investment advice—including investment newsletters and tip sheets—was widely (and erroneously) estimated to be in the thousands, no one from those groups came forward. As a result, witnesses were limited to SEC officials and representatives of a small number of advisers.

Professor Edwin Merrick Dodd testified in support of regulation of the investment counsel profession

Most of the advisers opposed the SEC's regulatory plan. The only surprise came during an appearance by E. Merrick Dodd, a professor at Harvard Law School. He had been invited to discuss the investment company scandals, but while waiting to testify he heard witnesses testifying on issues related to advisers, and he volunteered to weigh in on that subject as well.

> I have been somewhat astonished as I have been listening to the testimony today and read the testimony of yesterday, at the suggestion that because investment advisers, investment counsel, properly enough regard themselves as members of a profession, that is the reason why they should not be regulated. It seems to me quite obvious that just the opposite is the case, that it is the normal practice under our laws, both state and federal, to regulate professions; when people hold themselves out as competent to render professional services to the public we do regulate them. We regulate the profession to keep undesirable people out. We regulate the legal profession, we regulate the medical profession, we regulate the accounting profession, and we regulate all of the major professions.[22]

Dodd's brief comments helped convince any committee members who still might have had reservations that investment advisers should be included in the reform legislation.

A compromise came when industry representatives opposing the bill began to realize that some legislation was politically inevitable. At the same time, the SEC felt the strain of more than three years of investment company hearings and was now facing congressionally mandated deadlines for reform proposals. Both sides were thus open to compromise, and the SEC made the first move. Hardwick Stires, a Scudder Stevens executive attending some of the Senate hearings, shared a cab after one of the sessions with Schenker, who got directly to the point, as Stires later recalled. "Wicks, don't you fellows think it's time to throw in the sponge and realize there is going to be a bill and that we are going to have, as a minimum, a registration of investment counsel?" Stires later recalled Schenker asking him. "So why don't you tell your group to stop thrashing and get together and write a simple bill that I feel sure we can all agree on?"[23]

Stires and his colleagues jumped at the offer. The next evening, several industry representatives and Robert G. Page, a lawyer from

GLASS-STEAGALL ACT OF 1933:
Prohibited most securities activities by commercial banks. Separated commercial banking from investment banking. Part of the Banking Act of 1933, which also established the federal deposit insurance.

SECURITIES ACT OF 1933:
Regulated the issuance of securities by requiring the registration of new offerings and the full disclosure of financial information. Prohibited misrepresentation or other fraud in the sale of securities.

SECURITIES AND EXCHANGE ACT OF 1934: Established the Securities and Exchange Commission with broad authority to regulate the securities industry, markets, and trading. Required broker-dealers to register with the SEC and comply with its rules.

PUBLIC UTILITY HOLDING COMPANY ACT OF 1935: Enacted to address fraud, stock manipulation, and other abuses that had led to the collapse of major utility companies. In accordance with this act, Congress ordered the SEC to investigate investment companies for their role in financing the utility manipulations.

MALONEY ACT OF 1938: Authorized self-regulatory organizations to police the securities industry under the direction of the SEC. Led to 1939 designation of the National Association of Securities Dealers as a self-regulatory organization for the securities industry.

INVESTMENT COMPANY ACT OF 1940: Established regulatory framework for mutual funds, also known as investment companies or investment trusts. Required registration with the SEC and full disclosure of relevant information.

INVESTMENT ADVISERS ACT OF 1940: Required registration of investment advisers with the SEC and imposed antifraud provisions on their activities. Banks and broker-dealers were generally exempted from registration.

President Franklin Roosevelt
signs the Glass-Steagall
Act of 1933

New York, began an all-night drafting session to prepare the bill Schenker had requested. The new bill had the registration and antifraud provisions sought by the SEC, as well as restrictions on adviser contract assignments and principal trading by advisers with clients. It also featured a measure sought by the industry making it unlawful for registered advisers to use the term *investment counsel* unless they were primarily engaged in the business of rendering "continuous advice as to the investment of funds on the basis of the individual needs of the client." The bill was accepted with only slight change by the SEC and passed both the Senate and the House without significant modification. What became the Investment Advisers Act of 1940 took up just three pages when reprinted in the *Congressional Record.* By contrast, the Investment Company Act of 1940 required thirty pages.

a course for the future

For a law that seemed in many respects an afterthought at the time of its passage, the Investment Advisers Act of 1940 has proven remarkably practical and enduring, both for the investing public and for the advisory industry.[24] Several factors have contributed to its success. One is the emphasis on full disclosure. The Advisers Act is at its heart a disclosure statute. Registered investment advisers are required to disclose real and potential conflicts of interest to their clients. Over the years, the SEC has expanded the scope of its disclosure requirements, and even put a key disclosure document, part 1 of Form ADV, online so it can be viewed conveniently over the Internet by the public.

A second factor has been the SEC's broad and flexible authority to regulate fraud in the industry. Though the final draft of the legislation was written by the Investment Counsel Association of America, the industry's only trade group at the time, its role turned out not to be a drawback. The ICAA's standards of practice were exemplary, and the legislation confirmed and codified them. By ceding regulatory power to the SEC, the ICAA demonstrated its commitment to ethical practices and its intolerance for unscrupulous conduct.

Most important in the long run has been the way the law was later interpreted by the U.S. Supreme Court. In *SEC. v. Capital Gains Research Bureau, Inc.*, the high court ruled that the 1940 Advisers Act "reflects a congressional recognition of the delicate fiduciary nature of an investment advisory relationship." The court also noted that the 1940 Advisers Act reflects "a congressional intent *to eliminate, or at least expose, all conflicts of interest* which might incline an investment adviser—consciously or unconsciously—to render advice which was not disinterested" (emphasis added). Further, the court said that every investment adviser owes his or her clients a duty of "utmost good faith, and full and fair disclosure of all material facts" as well as an affirmative obligation "to employ reasonable care to avoid misleading clients."[25]

The notion that the interest of the client must always come first has been strengthened over the years by subsequent court decisions and by SEC rule making. As the SEC noted in a 1988 analysis of the law:

> The act's imposition on the adviser of a fiduciary duty to clients is intended to eliminate conflicts of interest and to prevent the adviser from overreaching or taking unfair advantage of a client's trust. An adviser, as a fiduciary, owes clients more than honesty and good faith alone. An adviser must also be sensitive to the possibility of rendering less than disinterested advice whether consciously or unconsciously, and an adviser may be faulted even where it did not intend to injure the client and even if the client does not suffer a monetary loss.[26]

Original Investment Counsel Association of America *Code of Professional Practice*, published in 1937

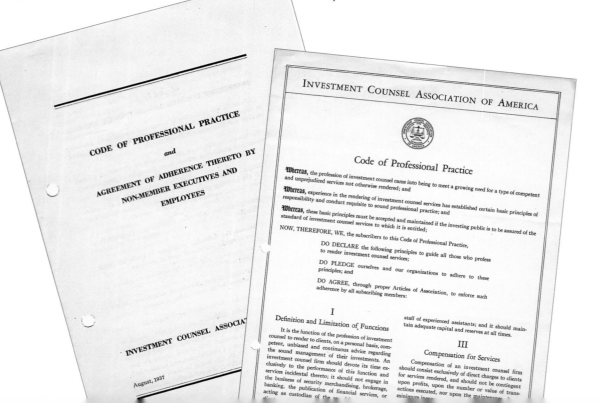

CODE OF PROFESSIONAL PRACTICE

and

AGREEMENT OF ADHERENCE THERETO BY NON-MEMBER EXECUTIVES AND EMPLOYEES

INVESTMENT COUNSEL ASSOCIA

August, 1937

INVESTMENT COUNSEL ASSOCIATION OF AMERICA

Code of Professional Practice

Whereas, the profession of investment counsel came into being to meet a growing need for a type of competent and unprejudiced services not otherwise rendered; and

Whereas, experience in the rendering of investment counsel services has established certain basic principles of responsibility and conduct requisite to sound professional practice; and

Whereas, these basic principles must be accepted and maintained if the investing public is to be assured of the standard of investment counsel services to which it is entitled;

NOW, THEREFORE, WE, the subscribers to this Code of Professional Practice,

DO DECLARE the following principles to guide all those who profess to render investment counsel services;

DO PLEDGE ourselves and our organizations to adhere to these principles; and

DO AGREE, through proper Articles of Association, to enforce such adherence by all subscribing members:

I

Definition and Limitation of Functions

It is the function of the profession of investment counsel to render to clients, on a personal basis, competent, unbiased and continuous advice regarding the sound management of their investments. An investment counsel firm should devote its time exclusively to the performance of this function and services incidental thereto; it should not engage in the business of security merchandising, brokerage, banking, the publication of financial services, or acting as custodian of the

staff of experienced assistants; and it should maintain adequate capital and reserves at all times.

III

Compensation for Services

Compensation of an investment counsel firm should consist exclusively of direct charges to clients for services rendered, and should not be contingent upon profits, upon the number or value of transactions executed, nor upon the maintenance of a minimum

Enacted to cover a relative handful of practitioners, the act today applies to many thousands of investment advisers. It was the first set of regulations to shape the fledgling profession, and a harbinger of the three decades to come, during which investment advisers would begin to assume their modern role.

THREE

Stirrings Beneath the Surface

OR THE U.S. ECONOMY as a whole, World War II was a beneficial stimulus that put an end to the Great Depression. For investors and their advisers, however, the war years and the three decades that followed were stagnant. "On balance," writes Charles Geisst in his comprehensive history of Wall Street, "the situation in 1940 was as bad as at any time during the early years of the Depression."[1] To support the war effort, Americans enthusiastically bought bonds, but not stocks. There were few new stock offerings and few investment advisers around to recommend them: like other Americans of conscription age, they had joined the armed services in droves. Even New York Stock Exchange president William McChesney Martin, discouraged by the slow pace of business and increasing pressure from the Securities and Exchange Commission, answered a draft call early in the war. The sudden shortage of men in the investment adviser community opened the doors—at least temporarily—to talented women such as Scudder's Margaret Ogden, who'd begun her career as a librarian and who rose during the war to become the firm's first female research analyst.

The end of the war ushered in an unprecedented boom of rising incomes, record consumer spending, increased factory output, and a sustained bull market. Yet between 1940 and 1970 the financial

The U.S. entry into World War II depleted the ranks of invest-ment advisers

William McChesney Martin served as the first full-time salaried president of the New York Stock Exchange from 1938 to 1941

services industry itself, and the makeup and perspective of investors, changed very little from the early years of the century. With employers almost universally taking care of workers' retirement funding through pensions, average Americans preferred to plow their hard-earned cash into real estate and life insurance rather than "speculate" in stocks. The stock market remained, as it had for decades, the province of the very wealthy.

But that's not to say the years between 1940 and 1970 were an uneventful lull for the investment adviser community. On the contrary, the fledgling industry was being dynamically molded by two forces: one external, the other internal.

From the outside, the SEC increased its regulatory power over the financial services industry in general and, increasingly, over investment advisers. The process began with the passage of the Investment Advisers Act of 1940 and took a full three decades to assume its modern form.

And from the inside, investment advisers began to create the means to regulate and educate themselves. The result would be a new profession that emerged in the early 1970s: financial planning.

an industry reveals itself

The Investment Advisers Act of 1940 required advisers to register with the Securities and Exchange Commission for the first time in history.

But the act didn't tell the SEC what to do with those registrations. True, the new law gave SEC lawyer David Schenker, who had led the agency's 1936–39 investigations into the activities of investment companies and investment advisers, a mandate to clean up the scandal-ridden investment companies, known today as mutual funds. But his authority over advisers was less specific and involved mostly information gathering—itself an important first step toward regulation. During the previous decade's investigations, Schenker and his SEC colleagues had been frustrated by their inability to gather information about investment advisers, almost all of them small, independent organizations. Now that information began arriving in Washington.

But if Schenker had expected a torrent, he was soon disappointed. In 1937, *Newsweek* magazine estimated there were five thousand investment advisers nationwide. Schenker and others had testified in congressional hearings that the number was at least six thousand. Both estimates turned out to be wildly inflated. Late in 1940, Schenker told a meeting of the Investment Counsel Association of America (ICAA), the leading trade association for advisers, that only 895 applications had been received for adviser registration.

In his talk, Schenker entertained the audience by describing some of the rejected registrants. One claimed on his registration form to have had years of experience in the oil and gold-mining industries. His clients, he declared, benefited significantly from his expertise in the stock and bond markets. "Every known [sic] in the investment field is considered in order to insure the client the maximum profit and the maximum safety," the applicant wrote. When the SEC followed up on these bold claims, it located the man in a Wisconsin prison where he was serving time for assault. The convict's objective, Schenker said, had been "to show the parole board he had a business to go to as soon as he was released."[2] Needless to say, this self-described expert was not among the advisers granted registration in 1940. In fact, the total number of registrations came to only seven hundred, which meant the agency rejected roughly 20 percent of the registration forms it received. Clearly, the adviser industry was much smaller and less influential than the SEC had envisioned. Developing a formal regulatory scheme hardly seemed worth the effort.

Besides, the new regulators lacked the tools to monitor the dealings between investment adviser firms and their clients. The registration form, though long, provided only a general picture of each advisory firm. For example, of the 895 firms filing applications for registration, 367 were sole proprietorships. Schenker found this large proportion grounds for concern. In his remarks to the ICAA, he worried that these one-man shops might be fly-by-night operations without even an established place of business. Yet the SEC had no authority to conduct even routine examinations. And even if it had had the authority, because the law contained no provision requiring advisers to keep books and records, there might be nothing to examine. If it suspected outright fraud, the SEC had the power to act. But its lack of oversight power greatly limited its effectiveness.

It would take a couple of decades for investment advisers to become numerous and influential enough to attract serious regulatory attention. The industry was growing, but very slowly. Each year between 1940 and 1970 fewer than a hundred firms joined the ranks of registered advisers. In 1950 there were barely a thousand investment adviser firms. In 1970 that number had increased to just thirty-five hundred. The majority of investment advisers continued to cater to the financial elite; the most prominent styled themselves as investment counsel, typically providing fee-based advice to wealthy, sophisticated individuals and institutions that was not subject to the same conflicts as commission-based advice provided by broker-dealers. Not until the 1980s, when investment markets opened to working- and middle-class Americans and technological innovation and entrepreneurial wealth dramatically changed the financial landscape, would the community of investment advisers experience significant growth—and change.

building a modern regulatory structure

As World War II drew to a close, the SEC pressed Congress to grant the agency the expanded powers it needed. First on the list was the ability to require advisers to keep books and records and the authority to routinely examine them. In a special report to Congress in 1945, the agency proposed those measures and others to beef up the original 1940 legislation. But Congress's attention lay elsewhere, and the proposals languished for years. They were reintroduced in

It would take a couple of decades for investment advisers to become numerous and influential enough to attract serious regulatory attention.

1957 and again in 1959, when the House Special Subcommittee on Legislative Oversight pronounced: "It is time in view of the increasing public reliance upon investment advisers, to strengthen the Act and make it more than a mere census of persons in the investment advisory business."

In addition to the record-keeping and examination provisions, new amendments authorized the agency to require the reporting of securities transactions by advisory personnel and to regulate advertising by advisers. The SEC now could deny registration to advisers convicted of financial crimes, embezzlement, or violations of securities laws. The agency was empowered to suspend the registration of advisers for up to twelve months; previously the only legal sanction was revocation of the adviser's registration. The SEC could promulgate rules aimed at preventing fraud, even among advisers who were not registered with the SEC because they were exempt or had failed to comply with the registration requirements. The amendments also helped eliminate potential conflicts with state regulation of advisers and endorsed the concept of concurrent state and federal jurisdiction over them. At last, the SEC had additional tools to enforce the provisions of the Advisers Act. In 1963, more than two decades after the law's passage, the agency started conducting routine examinations of investment adviser firms.

All along, though, the SEC had been fighting adviser fraud through rule making, interpretive orders, and enforcement actions, with mixed results. The most famous enforcement action was its 1963 case against Capital Gains Research Bureau, the name of both a registered

adviser and of that adviser's investment newsletter publisher. The firm had secretly bought shares of stocks it was about to recommend to its five thousand newsletter subscribers and to a much larger mailing list of prospective customers. Stock prices rose after the newsletters were mailed, and the company sold out at a quick profit.

The SEC brought an action in federal district court in New York for an injunction to force the company to disclose or discontinue the practice, which it alleged to be a fraud on investors. As one observer reported, "To the amazement of the financial community, the District Court of the Southern District of New York refused to grant the injunction, and to its greater astonishment the Circuit Court of Appeals for the Second Circuit in its turn sustained the lower court."[3] In 1963 the SEC appealed the case to the U.S. Supreme Court, which reversed the previous decisions. The high court ruled that the publisher's actions constituted fraud under the Advisers Act. It backed the SEC's bid to require disclosure of such activities to clients, and even called that remedy "mild." Most important, it affirmed that the original statute held investment advisers to strict fiduciary standards in their dealings with clients.[4] It was a landmark victory for the SEC that greatly strengthened the Commission's legal powers. Advisers celebrated, too: the entire industry benefited from the tougher stance on fraud.

On the legislative front, Congress in 1963 received the report of a special commission, chaired by Chicago lawyer Milton H.

Milton Cohen (center)
and members of the 1963
SEC special study group
that recommended
securities reforms

Cohen, which had been created to come up with securities reform recommendations. Among those recommendations: the creation of a self-regulatory organization, or SRO, for investment advisers. It was the first of many times when that idea would be floated—so far unsuccessfully because of strong industry opposition. (Not that the concept is without precedent. For some time, broker-dealers have been subject to oversight by self-regulatory organizations such as the New York Stock Exchange and the National Association of Securities Dealers, which in turn are subject to SEC oversight.) The commission also wanted the SEC to set professional standards for advisory firm personnel and suggested that a national board of securities examiners administer licensing programs. The SEC was receptive to an SRO for advisers; the investment adviser industry was not. As a result, Congress shelved the SRO proposal and the commission's other reforms.

The reformers won the next round in 1970, when Congress approved a new set of amendments to the Advisers Act. These amendments strengthened the SEC's authority to discipline advisers and advisory firm personnel and expanded the agency's ability to grant exemptions from the act's provisions. The amendments also allowed advisers to charge high-net-worth clients performance fees—known as "fulcrum fees"—in certain circumstances,

generally when portfolio performance exceeded an index or other benchmark.

Throughout the 1950s, 1960s, and 1970s, the SEC's interest in strengthening its control over investment advisers ebbed and flowed. Periods of relatively little regulatory activity were followed by intervals of crackdowns to address particular industry problems. When it wanted to fill gaps in its regulatory authority, the agency often had to wait years for Congress to address the issues; sometimes no new authority was granted. And when a reform package did pass, the next one was unlikely to succeed until a good deal of time had elapsed. Thus, a reform plan proposed in 1976, just six years after the previous set of amendments, probably would have faced an uphill struggle in any event. The proposals would have dramatically expanded the SEC's authority over advisers, establishing professional qualification standards for advisers and requiring them to meet minimum financial responsibility standards. Hugh F. Owens, an SEC commissioner, had pushed for both measures. "As much or more than the clients of broker-dealers," he said, "the clients of investment advisers seem to rely on the professional competence of their advisers, and the absence of qualification requirements for investment advisers and persons associated with them constitutes an undesirable gap in the pattern of federal securities regulation."[5]

But critics said the SEC was unable to justify its case. "No evidence of need was developed at the hearings or presented to the committee by the SEC," said Sen. Jesse Helms, R-North Carolina.[6]

Appointed by President Lyndon Johnson, SEC Commissioner Hugh F. Owens (second from left) pushed for measures to expand the SEC's authority over advisers

A subsequent attempt in 1989 to establish an SRO for investment advisers met a similar fate.

Another major change to the Advisers Act came in 1996 with the passage of the Investment Advisers Supervision Coordination Act, part of a larger measure known as the National Securities Markets Improvement Act. It reduced the SEC's workload by giving the states jurisdiction over advisers with $25 million or less in assets under management. As a result, the SEC's resources were freed up to concentrate on regulating larger advisory firms, while the states focused on smaller ones. The change was intended to boost the overall effectiveness of federal and state supervisory efforts and ease burdens on firms operating in more than one state.

"The Coordination Act represents a grand experiment in new federalism," David G. Tittsworth, executive director of the Investment Advisers Association, testified after the law had taken effect. "By and large we believe the results have been successful in achieving the objectives of the legislation."[7]

Other new SEC rules in recent years have strengthened or streamlined adviser regulation. Among them were changes to the registration Form ADV filed each year by advisers, the introduction of electronic ADV filing, and the subsequent launch of the online Form ADV database in 2000.[8] The Commission also required advisers to establish policies and procedures regarding the voting of proxies and to provide information to clients about how proxies are voted,[9] and it modernized rules regarding the custody of client assets in order to combat fraud.[10] More recently, the 2004 mutual fund trading scandals prompted new requirements that advisory firms adopt procedures designed to prevent violations of the federal securities laws, designate chief compliance officers, and adopt codes of ethics.[11]

In retrospect, the unsuccessful 1976 amendments represented the SEC's most vigorous efforts to expand its regulatory mandate over investment advisers. Today's regulatory landscape for investment advisers was shaped almost entirely by the 1940 act, the amendments of 1960 and 1970, subsequent SEC rules resulting from those legislative acts, and related court decisions.

LOREN DUNTON, THE FATHER OF PERSONAL FINANCIAL PLANNING

Central Casting couldn't have found a more apt or colorful candidate than Loren Dunton to play the role of industry pioneer. Dunton was born in 1918 in the small mining town of Trail, British Columbia, near the Washington State border and very far from Wall Street. According to one biographical note, "he enjoyed an exciting bachelor life in Seattle, Alaska, and San Francisco" before marrying his first wife at twenty-nine. He took up parachuting at age forty-five, the same year he published his first book, *Self-Discipline;* twelve more books—including *How to Sell to Women, Your Book of Financial Planning,* and *Prime Time: How to Enjoy the Best Years of Your Life*—would follow.

Above all, Dunton was a salesman and a promoter with a strong streak of idealism. He sold vacuum cleaners and encyclopedias before settling in Colorado, where he sold mutual funds and started a consulting firm whose clients were financial service providers. While working with them, Dunton came to see the need for higher standards of professionalism in retail financial services. He formed the Society for Financial Counseling Ethics and began looking for a way to bring his ideas to a larger audience. He found his messenger in a local life insurance salesman, James R. Johnston, who had long enjoyed listening to motivational speakers but felt frustrated by their lack of follow-through. Johnston recognized Dunton's motivational talents and offered himself as the educator who would take up where Dunton left off.

Together, the two men planned a national summit to create a professional organization for financial advisers that would offer education and certification. Yet despite his considerable skills as a connector, Dunton was able to persuade only eleven financial professionals to come to Chicago on December 12, 1969, and participate in what is now considered a signal event in financial planning history.

The International Association for Financial Planning and its educational wing, the College for Financial Planning, struggled for several years under Dunton's leadership before eventually becoming important contributors to the financial planning industry. Dunton gave up the helm of the IAFP in 1974 and eventually moved to San Francisco, where he continued his public-speaking and writing careers. He founded several nonprofit groups, including the National Center for Financial Education, which taught consumers how to have a secure financial future. Dunton died in 1997 at age 79.

> Dunton came to see the need for higher standards of professionalism in retail financial services.

"the world was ripe for financial planning"

Although independent advisers resisted external pressures to form a self-regulatory organization, that didn't mean they were indifferent to professional standards. On the contrary, by the late 1960s they showed a mounting interest in education and certification. J. Chandler Peterson, an industry pioneer and early president of the International Association for Financial Planning, later described it as a kind of collective awakening. "All across the country, in the late 1960s and early 1970s, people were arriving at the same ideas independently but simultaneously," he said. "It just took something to flush the ideas out."[12]

That "something" took place in Chicago on December 12 and 13, 1969. Loren Dunton, a Colorado financial consultant, and James R. Johnston, a life-insurance salesman, had persuaded eleven colleagues from the securities, mutual fund, and insurance industries to meet at a hotel near O'Hare Airport to talk about dramatically improving the level of professionalism in retail financial services and replacing salesmanship with "financial counseling" as the industry's driving force. The attendees included salesmen of mutual funds and securities and life insurance; one was a financial counselor, one was a publicist. They came from Florida, New York, Ohio, and Pennsylvania; most paid their own expenses. When they left Chicago the following day, the foundation had been laid for two organizations: the International Association for Financial Planning and its educational wing, the College for Financial Planning. In addition, Dunton soon conceived the idea of a certification program for financial counselors, the Certified Financial Planner™ (CFP®) designation.

Why did the financial planning movement emerge at this time? The best way to answer the question is to look at what had come before. Here's how industry veterans E. Denby Brandon Jr., and H. Oliver Welch, writing in 2003, set the scene:

> Between 1945 and 1970, the mainstream of the financial services field generally continued to serve clients in a fragmented way. As a result, many clients had financial programs characterized by lack of balance and adequate diversification. They were largely determined by the professional training and compensation of the person who had the most influence with the client. For example,

if a good life insurance salesman had the most impact on the client's financial life, more attention would usually be given to estate or death planning and the purchase of whole life insurance. A good securities salesman would direct the client's attention to life-time or investment planning and the purchase of securities recommended by his firm. Real estate, tax shelter or hard-assets salespeople would all tend to impose their products on the client's financial activities. In many cases, a turf-protection mentality would prevent the various salespeople from seeking more appropriate solutions to their clients' financial problems.[13]

Clearly, financial planners believed that product sales was not an appropriate driver for client advice. Someone who had no interest in promoting specific products was needed to take a chair on the client's side of the table and offer objective advice. This adviser would make recommendations based on the client's goals and circumstances, not the level of product commissions.

Some key concepts of financial planning—but not the term "financial planning"—were used by investment counsel firms as early as the 1920s. Those firms made an effort to understand a client's circumstances and financial goals in order to recommend an appropriate course of action. They also monitored the client's investment portfolio. These practices—which were fully consonant with what emerged in the 1960s and 1970s as financial planning—were codified to some extent in the Investment Advisers Act of 1940, the regulatory regime that applied most closely to the emerging financial planning industry.

Nevertheless, whatever its debt to early investment-counsel firms, financial planning evolved most directly from the life insurance industry. "As late as 1960, life insurance was the substance of financial planning," said Rich White, an early chronicler of the profession. At that time, "By definition, a financial planner was an insurance man who offered the public more than money-if-you-die. Financial planners . . . estimated estate tax payments for wealthy customers and sold insurance to fund those payments. They formed clinics in which they analyzed financial goals and sold packages of life insurance, disability insurance and annuities."[14]

The term for this methodology was "needs-based selling." To figure the amount of life insurance or disability insurance required by a client, the agent analyzed the family's financial objectives and future

Someone who had no interest in promoting specific products was needed to take a chair on the client's side of the table . . .

spending needs, then subtracted existing financial resources. The present value of the shortfall was the amount of insurance recommended by the agent.[15] This now much evolved capital needs analysis approach, often using sophisticated sensitivity analyses and Monte Carlo simulation, is routinely used by financial planners to explore client financial goals. "The approach of looking at the client's needs was clearly derived from the life insurance industry," said Dr. William L. Anthes, retired president of the College for Financial Planning. "But the life insurance people tried to solve *every* problem through life insurance. Although some founders of the financial planning industry came out of the life insurance business, they were saying there's got to be another way to solve a person's problem."

Dunton had already reached this conclusion. "Dunton knew from his experience in sales training that the world was ripe for financial planning," wrote one observer a decade after the Chicago meeting. "The concept would simply sell itself once he, the promoter, got the ball rolling."[16]

And Dunton was the best kind of promoter: one who believed fervently in what he was offering. "Many pressures are being exerted on the consumer to spend, but there had been no effort on the part of the financial services industry to counteract these forces. People weren't compelled to save or allocate their monies wisely," he later observed. The Society for Financial Counseling Ethics, which Dunton had founded in mid-1969, "was formed in large part to compete with advertisers and marketers who were urging people to spend," he added. "Its mission was to educate Americans as to why they should save, insure, invest their money, and plan for retirement."[17]

Like many entrepreneurs, Dunton—who is credited with coining the term *certified financial planner*—was more successful launching projects than sustaining them. The early rush of enthusiasm with which his ideas were greeted was soon replaced by a torrent of challenges. "None of [the participants in the Chicago area] had the financial clout to reach into the deep pockets of the many wealthy corporations in the financial services field," wrote Brandon and Welch. "To begin these two organizations they had a totally inadequate amount of current capital, only a vague action plan, and no one with real organizational experience to undertake projects of this magnitude. There were no outstanding educators or educational institutions represented. It is difficult to imagine a major movement in the financial services field with the odds so heavily stacked against its success."[18]

The shining exception to this bleak picture was the College for Financial Planning, which controlled the CFP mark and set educational standards for its attainment. In charge of the college's planning was Lewis G. Kearns, director of financial planning for Wellington Management Company, a money management firm located in Boston and known for its flagship Wellington Fund. He recruited the Chicago meeting's co-organizer, James R. Johnston, who had a background in life insurance and a burning interest in education. Both men were inspired leadership choices. By the time the college opened its doors in Denver in 1972, dozens of students had enrolled in its first class.

But the college faced a serious problem: financial planning was virtually virgin territory. There were few targeted textbooks or course materials for the new discipline. It was not taught anywhere else. In fact no one had formally defined the scope or methodology of financial planning. The creation of the college's curriculum would represent the creation of the new profession's intellectual capital.

Johnston, who later became the college's president, took on this Herculean task with zeal. With long-distance advice from Kearns, he planned and wrote the seventeen chapters of "Counseling the Individual," the first course that the first class of students would take. Johnston researched and wrote feverishly, keeping one step ahead of the students as their coursework progressed. The college would later use the motto "We wrote the book on financial planning." It's more accurate to say that James R. Johnston wrote the book on financial planning.[19]

The College for Financial Planning became independent of the Society for Financial Counseling Ethics in 1972 and obtained nonprofit status in 1973. That year, forty-two students graduated as the industry's first CFP professionals. By the end of the decade, there were approximately twenty-one hundred CFP professionals. "The emergence of the CFP designation," wrote Gail Quint in her history of the college, "began to chip away at the public perception that all financial representatives were salespeople interested chiefly in the accumulation of sales commissions in a product-oriented industry versus a view of professionals interested in a consumer-service and planning function."[20]

This house in Denver was one of the first offices of the College for Financial Planning

The first graduating class of the College for Financial Planning in 1973

Among those who took note of the new professional designation was the National Association of Securities Dealers, and its former president, Gordon S. Macklin. In October 1972, the NASD issued a notice to all member firms warning about broker-dealer representatives using terms such as *financial planning, financial counseling,* or *financial consultant.* The notice cited an SEC action in which a broker-dealer had been found in violation of antifraud rules because employees represented themselves as "financial planning experts" when they were not. An attorney at the SEC, Ezra Weiss, reviewed the NASD Notice to Members and convinced his boss, SEC chairman William Casey (later to become director of the Central Intelligence Agency), that the CFP mark was deceptive and had to be abolished. He proposed Certified Financial Representative (CFR) as an appropriate replacement. Casey happened to be a friend of Ferdinand Nauheim, chairman of the board of trustees of the College for Financial Planning; he asked Nauheim to change the mark. "The day I learned of the problem I called him," Nauheim said later. "He said, 'Ferd, I'm having a sardine sandwich and a glass of milk on my desk. Get yourself a sandwich and join me.'" Nauheim hurried over.[21]

Eventually Nauheim relented. He persuaded the college's trustees to change the CFP mark to CFR—and started a firestorm of protest. Though still tiny, the financial planning community had become attached to the CFP mark and didn't want to see it polluted or watered down. (The episode foreshadowed a similar controversy over a proposal three decades later to create an Associate CFP designation, dubbed CFP Lite by detractors.) But before push could come

to shove, Nauheim, Weiss, and Casey all left their respective jobs, and the issue was dropped.

The CFP mark may have been safe, but the College for Financial Planning remained intermittently short of funds for some time, its future continually precarious. Johnston, now the college president, fought to keep the new institution alive. "We were always flying by the seat of our pants, struggling to meet great challenges," he recalled later. "There was a lot of skepticism on the part of out-siders who said it couldn't be done. But people kept enrolling—or returning after they'd dropped out." The bottom came at the end of 1974, when it appeared the college would be unable to meet its year-end payroll. On Christmas Eve, a desperate Johnston began calling contacts at large organizations that sponsored groups of students for the CFP designation. He got through to Jay Hines, an executive at IDS Corporation, a financial services firm with a finan-cial planning–based marketing approach. (IDS was later purchased by American Express.) IDS had fifty-one students enrolled. Could he help? Hines immediately offered to prepay his students' tuition, which solved the college's short-term cash crisis. "After that, I knew it all had to work out," Johnston said later.[22]

The tide had turned, although success did not occur overnight. By 1979, when William Anthes became the College's third presi-dent—a post he held through 1992—the institution still "had a number of problems," in Anthes's words. "But I also witnessed the commitment of the students who wanted to become CFP profes-sionals and enter that new field of financial planning." Under Anthes, the college would experience dynamic growth, greatly improve the quality of its offerings, and become accredited.

Even bigger changes were on the horizon in the second half of the 1970s and throughout the 1980s, not just for the CFP mark and financial planners but for the entire independent investment adviser profession. On the negative side: out-of-control inflation and roller-coasting boom-and-bust markets. On the positive side: revolutionary changes in retirement regulation. Together, these forces were about to transform the way in which middle-class Americans looked at investing and retirement planning—and the way in which they got help with the increasingly difficult choices they were forced to make.

FOUR

Dark Clouds with a Silver Lining

TWO WEEKS AFTER Loren Dunton and his colleagues met in Chicago to launch the financial planning movement—which would dramatically change the scope of the independent advisory profession—President Richard Nixon signed into law a piece of legislation with an equally important effect on investors and their advisers. The Tax Reform Act of 1969, Nixon declared, represented "a sweeping revision" of the tax code: it would close loopholes that had allowed "far too many of our citizens to avoid the taxes that others have had to pay."

The act was indeed far-reaching. But it was not a panacea nor could it prevent the financial troubles on the horizon.

The social upheaval of the 1960s—which saw the Cold War, the Vietnam War, urban riots, and political assassinations—had been offset, paradoxically, by a financial boom. But as the 1970s dawned, the economic good times came sputtering to an end. Inflation turned to "stagflation," a newly minted term to describe the unprecedented combination of stagnant business activity, rising unemployment, and inflation. Loan rates soared, but interest on savings accounts stayed legally capped at low levels. Between 1970 and 1981, stocks languished in the worst bear market since the 1930s. In early 1973, the Organization of Petroleum Exporting Countries (OPEC), sharply

In 1969, President Nixon signed the most far-reaching tax bill since the enactment of the income tax in 1913

raised oil prices; in October of that year, OPEC imposed an oil embargo to punish the United States for supporting Israel in the Yom Kippur War. The price of a gallon of gas quadrupled, from 30 cents to $1.20, and desperate drivers waited in long lines at gas stations for limited supplies. Not surprisingly, by 1975 consumer confidence, as measured by the University of Michigan's sentiment index, plunged 40 percent from the decade's earlier high.

Yet there was a silver lining in the dark economic clouds. Motivated by difficult times, investors turned increasingly to the emerging financial planning profession. As Loren Dunton later observed, "One of the misconceptions prevalent in the 1970s was that people turned to financial planners in growing numbers because a growing number of people were calling themselves financial planners. While that may be partially true, people actually started turning to financial planners because of the growing complexity of their financial lives."[1]

There were other silver linings as well, innovations born of adversity. The debut in 1971 of money market mutual funds generally enabled savers to earn higher returns than those yielded by bank savings accounts. The remarkable growth of money market funds—from 8 percent of all mutual funds in 1975 to 37 percent in 1982—helped introduce millions of American savers to mutual fund investing.[2] The Employee Retirement Income Security Act of 1974 (ERISA) introduced safeguards for employee retirement plans and required that they be prudently managed. And on May 1, 1975, in an event known on Wall Street as "Mayday," the Securities and Exchange Commission abolished fixed pricing of brokerage commissions. One consequence was the emergence shortly thereafter of discount brokerage firms such as Charles Schwab & Co., Inc. which offered trades to customers at sharply reduced prices. In the years after Mayday, independent advisers and discount brokers developed mutually beneficial relationships, with brokerage firms providing execution, custody, and other back-office and related services that helped take independent advisers to a new level of success.

"an insidious thief"

Treasury Secretary William E. Simon (left) and Chairman Alan Greenspan of the Council of Economic Advisors report a "very significant increase" in November 1974 unemployment

During the 1960s consumer prices rose an average of 2.5 percent a year. By itself, that figure wasn't cause for alarm; previous ten-year periods had experienced similar inflation rates. But the averages belied serious weaknesses in the economy. Spending on the Vietnam War and President Lyndon Johnson's Great Society programs had generated deficits. And the effects began appearing at decade's end: the inflation rate jumped to 4.7 percent in 1968, then to 6.1 percent in 1969. Meanwhile, unemployment rose, economic growth retreated, and productivity fell. The 1973–74 bear market drove stock prices down by 40 percent; the market's recovery over the next few years was slow and uneven. For the decade of the 1970s, after adjusting for the value lost to inflation, stocks delivered a total return of *minus* 13.24 percent. The figure for government bonds was minus 16.01 percent. As economist J. Bradford De Long observed in his study of 1970s inflation, "The sustained elevation of annual inflation to the 5- and 10-percent-a-year range for a decade has no parallel in any other period of America's past history."[3]

The impact of 1970s inflation cannot be overstated. Retirees on fixed pensions despaired as their purchasing power shrank by half

President Ford urged Americans to "Whip Inflation Now" and show support by wearing "WIN" buttons

over the decade. Younger people worried about covering living expenses that were expected to triple or quadruple by the time they retired. President Gerald R. Ford, for his part, called for Americans to "Whip Inflation Now" by wearing WIN buttons—a futile attempt to encourage savings and disciplined spending.

Independent advisers and financial planners were affected as well. Indeed, inflation played an important and positive role in shaping their profession.

In 1969 August C. Hansch had founded Financial Profiles, a service bureau in Carlsbad, California, that gathered and processed client information to generate financial plans. (After a 1998 acquisition, the company became a leading provider of financial planning software.) In the 1970s, Hansch's planning methodology placed inflation front and center. Writing at the end of the decade, he called inflation "an insidious thief . . . made more dangerous by its quiet but inexorable destruction of our savings." His firm faced the "thief" squarely. "The first query on our questionnaire is, 'On a scale of one to nine, how concerned are you about making sure that your long-range investments keep pace with inflation?'"[4] Addressing their clients' fears and concerns about inflation helped Hansch and other early financial planners build the credibility of their new profession.

tax reform's unexpected consequences

Inflation wasn't the only concern of financial planners and independent advisers and their clients. The Tax Reform Act of 1969, the first modern legislation labeled as "tax reform," opened a Pandora's box of complications. The law established new tax rates and also introduced the alternative minimum tax (AMT), in effect a parallel income tax system with its own rates and rules. Targeted at a few wealthy taxpayers who took advantage of legitimate exemptions and deductions to zero out their taxable incomes, the AMT had an unexpectedly broad impact: it affected not only the wealthy few but also taxpayers whose taxable incomes were close enough that they *might* be subject to the AMT. Furthermore, because the AMT brackets weren't indexed for inflation, every year more taxpayers were swept into its system.

Seven years later, with the passage of the Tax Reform Act of 1976, Congress sent another strong signal. The first major legislative effort to crack down on tax shelters, the 1976 act disallowed tax deductions for losses on certain types of investments in which the investor had little or no economic risk. It also applied tight restrictions to deductions for home offices and vacation property rentals, and the proceeds from the exercise of stock options were classified as ordinary income instead of capital gains. The act's centerpiece was an overhaul of the estate tax: for the first time, estate and gift taxes were unified, and the new law mandated carryover basis for inherited property, which provoked a storm of protest.

Though the carryover-basis provision was canceled before it could go into effect, other changes in the estate and gift tax remained confusingly in place and many estate plans immediately became outdated. Once again, taxpayers' need for expert financial assistance suddenly increased beyond what many CPAs and tax attorneys could offer, and some taxpayers found themselves consulting financial planners, investment specialists, and estate planners. Other people needed substantially revised estate plans.

The 1976 act had indeed instituted reforms. But it also introduced a new level of complexity to many Americans' financial lives.

the rise and fall of tax shelters

As tax laws changed, inflation worsened, and returns from stocks and bonds remained in negative territory, some investors—even conservative investors—looked for a creative escape route. They thought they found one in limited partnerships that owned hard assets such as real estate or oil and gas. The partnerships' appeal was twofold: they were widely viewed as better inflation hedges than stocks, and they afforded tax write-offs that could be used to shelter other income. Partnerships appealed to salespeople as well—including some who called themselves financial planners—because they offered higher sales commissions than mutual funds.

As limited partnership sales became more popular, Congress grew concerned. After its initial assault on tax shelters in the Tax

President Reagan promotes the Tax Reform Act of 1986, which aimed to simplify the income tax code, broaden the tax base and eliminate many tax shelters

Reform Act of 1976, Congress repeatedly tightened restrictions on them through the early 1980s.[5] Finally, Congress decided to lower the boom once and for all. The landmark Tax Reform Act of 1986 made dramatic changes, collapsing the number of personal income tax brackets to two from fourteen, reducing the top personal tax rate to 28 percent from 46 percent, equalizing tax rates on income and capital gains, and subjecting a larger number of taxpayers to the alternative minimum tax. Most importantly to many financial planners and their clients, the law introduced "passive loss" rules that effectively prevented individual investors from taking tax-shelter deductions. The changes quickly put the tax-shelter industry out of business, while posing serious challenges to many financial planners as well.

The changes "drove out a whole element of the financial planning industry that was very, very different [from other planners]—folks who needed big commissions and who never would have survived advising clients about mutual funds," says Kurt Cerulli, president of Cerulli Associates, a financial industry research firm.

"why not a mutual fund?"

Those who stayed needed to recommend other investment products to their clients to replace tax-shelter partnerships. "As the commission-oriented advisers looked around for something else to sell," Peggy Ruhlin recalls, "mutual funds came to the forefront. At that time, load mutual funds were paying commissions of eight or eight and a half percent. It wasn't what they got on tax shelters, but it was better than nothing."

Financial planners and other independent advisers weren't unfamiliar with mutual funds, which had been a popular product during the bull market of the 1960s and which still represented the bulk of many client portfolios. But for fee-only advisers and planners, who did not accept commissions, mutual funds posed a challenge. They used no-load funds, which had to be bought and sold separately through the mail by the client from each fund family distributor. No centralized order execution or custody service was available. Commission-based planners, on the other hand, had access to their broker-dealer affiliate's trading and custody services to handle load funds for their clients.

Whatever their compensation base, planners turned to mutual funds after 1986 as their overwhelming investment of choice. "There were some people, as there are today, who managed individual stocks and bonds," says Harold Evensky of Evensky & Katz, an independent advisory firm based in Coral Gables, Florida. "But that wasn't a viable solution for most people. Mutual funds were the only realistic investment product for us."

Mutual funds weren't merely a "realistic" option: they also proved to be a remarkably successful one. Between 1970 and 2006, total assets invested in mutual funds grew more than two-hundred-fold, to $10 trillion.[6] At the end of 2006, *each* of the eleven biggest individual mutual funds was larger than the industry's entire $47.6 billion in assets in 1970.

The numbers are especially relevant for independent advisers, who have shown a preference for investing their clients' money in mutual funds. With so much at stake, independent advisers have a clear interest in prudent and effective fund industry management.

The story might have turned out differently if it hadn't been for an innovation that changed the future of investing for independent advisers and the clients they served. That innovation was the money market fund, and it was invented not by a government agency or a Wall Street powerhouse firm but by two financial consultants with a good idea.

First, though, some background. During the 1970s banks and savings and loans were prohibited from paying more than the rate designated by the Federal Reserve Bank—then 5.5 percent. Loan rates, on the other hand, had no caps. For corporations and institutions that could afford to buy them, money market instruments—such as commercial paper, Treasury bills, and bank certificates in denominations of $100,000 or more—were very attractive because, being unregulated, they could pay market rates. For small savers, the picture was very different: when interest rates rose above 5.5 percent, as they did during the 1970s, those small savers were stuck. Banks lent money at double-digit rates and returned only 5.5 percent in interest.

There was nothing to be done about it until Bruce R. Bent and Henry Brown, who owned their own small financial consulting company on Wall Street, fastened on the problem. Bent and Brown couldn't start a bank and pay higher rates. How could they invest savers' funds at market rates and offer a decent return?

Bent later described his epiphany: "I was at my desk, looked up at my partner and said, 'Why not a mutual fund?' I didn't know anything about mutual funds at the time, but I thought it could work. Everyone said it was impossible. . . . I read the regulations and nowhere did it say it couldn't be done. People simply lacked the imagination to make it happen."[7]

The world's first money market fund, which Bent and Brown called The Reserve Fund, launched in late 1971. It allowed investors to pool their money and make short-term investments in money-market instruments that paid 8 to 9 percent—a far better return than savers were getting on passbook accounts. The fund got off to a slow start, but that changed dramatically after the *New York Times* published a story about the venture on January 7, 1973, headlined "Overnight Mutual Funds for Surplus Assets." The following Monday, Bent and Brown fielded a hundred phone calls from people who

BRUCE R. BENT, CO-INVENTOR OF THE MONEY MARKET MUTUAL FUND

The co-inventor of the money market mutual fund grew up in modest circumstances, one of five children of a post office employee and cafeteria worker. Young Bruce Bent started working when he was nine, and was working full time by the time he was fourteen. He served in the Marine Corps and then earned degrees in economics and business. By 1971 he was 33 and working with Henry Brown in their two-person financial consulting business on Wall Street. Most of their clients lacked the $100,000 or so it took to buy high-yielding instruments such as commercial paper. So Bent and

Today, the fund is worth $40 billion and is ranked among the 25 largest mutual fund companies in the United States.

Brown invented the money market mutual fund, which allowed smaller investors to pool their money and enjoy the money market's higher returns. Brown put up $100,000 of his own money to start The Reserve Funds in 1971; Bent put up nothing, and earned only $11,000 in salary in the fund's first year. In its second year he earned nothing. The two men went shopping for shareholders, contacting 125 brokerage firms, insurers, and other prospects. None invested. "We were exhausted

financially and emotionally," Bent later told *Time* magazine.

Then came fame in the form of a January 1973 article in the *New York Times*. In less than a month the company's assets rocketed from $400,000 to $1.9 million. In 2005, Bruce Bent was named to *Financial Planning* magazine's Hall of Fame, recognizing the "26 entrepreneurs and investors whose achievements have shaped the business of financial advice." Today, Bent's company, The Reserve Funds, is worth more than $40 billion and is ranked among the 25 largest mutual fund companies in the United States. In addition to his position as chairman of the company, Bent is a popular speaker on financial topics.

Bruce R. Bent was honored by The American Museum of Financial History, an affiliate of the Smithsonian Institution, for the world's first money market mutual fund had read the story. "By the end of the month, the fund had $1.8 million in assets," one chronicler later wrote. "By the end of the year, it had $100 million. . . . The big mutual fund companies quickly introduced money funds. . . . Investing would never be the same."[8]

The success of money market mutual funds seems paradoxical. The funds were introduced at a time when many households had no interest in or knowledge about mutual fund investing. Moreover, most mutual funds invested solely in stocks (there were a few bond funds and balanced funds), and declining values had made the stock market unappealing. However, savers were clamoring for higher yields on cash desposits, and money market funds, whose return rates were in the high teens, were the only place for average investors to find them. While not guaranteed by the government, money market funds were relatively safe and highly liquid. Also reassuring was the fact that, unlike long-term stock and bond funds, money market fund shares remain at a stable value day by day. Money market funds attracted vast numbers of new customers to the mutual fund industry, and their growth persisted as yields rose throughout the late 1970s and early 1980s: By the end of 2006, money market mutual funds totaled $2.3 trillion, about a quarter of all mutual fund assets and roughly eight million times the amount of money in The Reserve Funds at the end of 1972.

For mutual fund companies, money market funds were a boon because, in industry jargon, they were "sticky": they helped retain customer assets as well as grow them. Previously, investors selling shares in stock or bond funds had to take their money out of

Overnight Mutual Funds for Surplus Assets

By ROBERT D. HERSHEY Jr.

Two young money managers at the Teachers Insurance and Annuity Association faced a nettlesome problem several years ago: how to get maximum return on money that was earmarked for mortgage loans, loans whose closing date could only rarely be predicted in advance.

They grappled with this cash flow situation as best they could but finally decided to try to turn it into a business opportunity for themselves, leaving Teachers, a pension fund for colleges.

Now, five years later, Henry B. R. Brown, 46 years old, and Bruce R. Bent, 35, have launched what they believe to be the ideal vehicle for many short-term investors.

It is called the Reserve Fund, Inc., a mutual fund designed "as a convenient alternative to the direct investment of temporary cash balances" that often are put into such money market instruments as Treasury bills, commercial paper, bankers' acceptances or certificates of deposit.

The fund, which will invest mainly in the longer-(one year)

Although the Reserve Fund, whose copyrighted prospectus was cleared by the Securities and Exchange Commission in late September, is still in its infancy, with assets of only about $1-million, it is one of the more visible of a number of recent attempts to improve cash management services.

The First National City Bank and the Chemical Bank have taken steps in this direction, though without a specific vehicle. Chemical is also the Reserve Fund's custodian and has made a line of credit available to meet possible concentrations in possible redemptions.

Merrill Lynch, Pierce, Fenner & Smith, Inc., the nation's biggest brokerage house, has made rapid progress in a program to put fixed-income specialists in about half its 200 branches. One of Merrill Lynch's specialists said recently that 1,700 new institutional accounts had been opened in the last year — "anybody smaller than what the guys like Salomon Brothers and the First Boston Corporation go after."

Many of these companies had been getting cash management advice from local banks, which the Merrill specialist said were

This fund is believed to be planning to invest largely in commercial paper and to involve the Morgan Guaranty Trust Company.

Blyth declined to explain its plans because it had not yet registered its fund with the S.E.C.

Mr. Brown and Mr. Bent of the Reserve Fund profess to be unworried that the field is rapidly becoming more crowded. One reason is the sheer size of the potential market.

While treasurers and investors of all variety have been engaged for a decade or more in applying sharper pencils to investment returns "the surface hasn't even been scratched," according to a Reserve Fund brochure.

In a recent interview at his office Mr. Bent held up a thumb and forefinger with about a half inch of space between them. "If we can get just that much of the market we'll do very well," he declared.

Besides corporations—and the Reserve Fund says it would not be surprised to find even some very large ones among its customers—it hopes to appeal to bank trust departments, other mutual funds, investment advis-

Specifically, investors in the Reserve Fund buy $100 shares in a pool of money—the unit price never changes since "dividends" are paid daily, usually in fractional shares. Although returns are called dividends they are actually interest and considered as such with none of the tax advantages of dividends.

The Reserve Fund has a sophisticated shareholder accounting system, one that permits investments for as little as one day.

Proceeds from redeemed shares are usually on deposit in the investor's bank the same day telephoned instructions are received. The credits are wired between the Chemical Bank and the customer's bank.

The fund will avoid investing in commercial paper, which it believes is more risky than C. D.'s while not necessarily providing a higher return.

In fact, it will merchandise the fund as a substitute for investors who now buy paper. It emphasizes that the Reserve Fund can eliminate various mechanical problems in directly buying short-term obligations. Among these it cites "scheduling maturities, investing in round lots, safeguarding receipt and delivery of securities, reinvesting, and

Money market funds growth 1975–2000 (in billions)

Assets: $3.70	Assets: $76.36	Assets: $498.34	Assets: $1,845.28
Funds: 36	Funds: 106	Funds: 741	Funds: 1,039
End of 1975	End of 1980	End of 1990	End of 2000

SOURCE: Investment Company Institute, *Mutual Fund Fact Book*, (Washington DC: 1992, 2004).

Long-term mutual funds growth 1940–2000

Decade ending in	Number of funds	Assets ($B)	% change in assets over decade
1940	68	0.5	—
1950	98	2.5	400
1960	161	17.0	580
1970	361	47.6	180
1980	564	134.8	183
1990	3,079	1,065.2	690
2000	8,155	6,964.7	554

SOURCE: Investment Company Institute, *Mutual Fund Fact Book*, (Washington, DC: 2004).

the fund industry and return it to bank or brokerage accounts. Now the proceeds could be placed in the fund family's money market fund, earn a market yield, and be conveniently redirected to another long-term fund investment at any time.

This advantage was especially beneficial to no-load fund companies that dealt directly with their customers. Seizing the opportunity, fund sponsors that had previously been specialized asset managers now positioned themselves as full-service investment providers.

Independent advisers and planners also benefited from the introduction of money market funds, which gave them another option to offer their clients. And they profited indirectly from another landmark event: the abolition of fixed brokerage commissions on May 1, 1975. *Time* magazine announced the upheaval in dramatic language: "To stockbrokers, Mayday means nothing less than the abolition of the system that has enriched them in good times and pulled many of them through during long periods of market slack. What is more, negotiated—or 'unfixed'—commissions will begin a drastic restructuring of the securities markets."[9] Actually, it was the securities industry, not the markets, that was transformed. Brokerage firms consolidated, discount brokers emerged for the first time, and new products and ways of business—including those offered by independent advisers—flourished in the more open, competitive environment.

On May 1, 1975, known on Wall Street as "Mayday," the Securities and Exchange Commission abolished fixed pricing of brokerage commissions

'Mayday' Forebodes Some Uncertainty for Wall Street

By ROBERT J. COLE

Today is historic for Wall Street. After 183 years, it embarks on an era of negotiated commission rates.

But instead of sensing history in the making, brokers for the most part had a feeling of not really knowing what perils lurked ahead.

Until Mayday—as the industry has called the day when rates would be unfixed—brokers had a fair idea of what to expect. Except for big customers, who enjoyed certain rate advantages, they set the rates almost everyone paid. Now, with rates free to move, brokers are worrying how freely they will move.

Many repeated a widely heard remark "T

That environment was also being transformed by seismic changes in the American way of retirement. The revolution had begun back in 1962, when Representative Eugene J. Keogh, a Democrat from New York, sponsored legislation to create a new retirement vehicle. What became known as Keogh plans gave self-employed people, partnerships, and other unincorporated businesses the same access to tax-advantaged retirement plans that only corporations had previously enjoyed.[10] Over the next two decades, further changes in retirement laws, especially those favoring self-directed or individually owned retirement vehicles, would prove beneficial to independent advisers, who saw them as a way to attract clients who needed planning, advice, and asset management in addition to retirement savings.

John B. Keeble III exemplified this entrepreneurial type of adviser. As a Vanderbilt College student in the early 1950s, he'd taken a part-time job selling life insurance. But when he was offered a full-time position, he turned it down. "At the time, most insurance companies used about a two-and-one-half percent factor," Keeble later wrote. "Retirement planning, through an insurance company, was grossly inadequate at that time."[11] Instead, Keeble became an attorney for the Internal Revenue Service, a post he left in the 1960s to open a firm in Atlanta called Financial Service Corp. Its mission: securities and insurance sales to fund Keogh plans. Rich White, a chronicler of the early financial planning profession, tells of how Keeble, a private pilot, "confined his market to the territory he could reach conveniently within a

Customers of discount brokers like Charles Schwab & Co., Inc. benefited from reduced commission rates resulting from "Mayday"

November 21, 1976
S.F. Sunday Examiner & Chronicle

Bargain brokers claim a boom

Charles R. Schwab in the midst of a typical cut-rater's bare-bones equipment

By Jack Miller
Business Editor

Shares Per Order	Price Per Share	Old NYSE Minimum Commission	Schwab & Co. Commission	$ You Save	% You Save
100	$15	$34.35	$24.00	$10.65	31%
200	20	77.00	48.00	29.00	38
500	25	204.31	100.00	104.31	51
1000	5	139.70	60.00	79.70	57

Sample charges by discounters in the Bay Area

one-day flight. To help sell his Keoghs, he filled out pages of client data and then fed the data through a computer to produce an automated financial plan. . . . At the height of its growth in the 1970s, Financial Service Corp. trained and employed hundreds of salesmen, who were to branch out and start dozens of new organizations in its mold."[12]

Keeble served as the second president of the International Association for Financial Counseling, which later became the International Association for Financial Planning. He advocated broadening the expertise of financial planners beyond a single discipline such as insurance sales with which they had typically started their careers. "Keeble . . . came to the conclusion that if a salesman were to sell both life insurance and mutual funds . . . in conjunction with a comprehensive financial plan, he would serve the consumer better," another history recounts.[13]

The Keogh plan had been targeted at self-employed individuals and small businesses. Other retirement-savings innovations had far more widespread implications. ERISA, enacted in 1974, tightened restrictions on defined benefit pensions, at the time the most common form of pension offered by corporations to employees. The Individual Retirement Account, or IRA, also created in 1974, permitted individuals not participating in employer retirement plans to set aside money each year, tax deferred, until they reached retirement age. And the employer-sponsored 401(k) plan, introduced in 1981, allowed employees to contribute up to 15 percent of their salary to the plan while deferring taxes on that money until it was taken out of the plan. The tide was shifting away from employer-funded retirement and toward today's defined-contribution model, in which workers take responsibility for their own retirement savings.

The numbers tell the story. Between 1982 and 1986, when IRAs were available and all workers younger than seventy and a half were eligible to make tax-deductible contributions, the amount contributed to IRAs jumped sharply, from $4.8 billion in 1981 to $38.2 billion in 1985.[14]

ERISA's landmark provisions were designed to help protect traditional defined-benefit pension plans, but the law's requirements actually helped contribute to a decline in their use. As more employees turned to self-directed or individually owned retirement vehi-

Representative Eugene J. Keogh, a Democrat from New York, sponsored legislation giving self-employed people, partnerships, and other unincorporated businesses access to tax-advantaged retirement plans

cles, independent advisers found their services in high demand. After all, participants in traditional defined-benefit plans need little or no advice. When they retire, they start receiving monthly checks; when they die, the checks cease. But 401(k) plan participants often need asset allocation and investment selection advice. And rollover IRAs, which eventually serve as the collection points for 401(k) assets, are fully under the ownership and control of the account holder. Account holders find they need investment advice during the accumulation years, and they need even more advice on arcane distribution regulations during the withdrawal years—even if they haven't sought investment advice in the past.

"Our research shows that people actually act differently about their retirement money than they do about their other investments," says David Hunt, a director of McKinsey & Company. "Historically there's been an argument in the industry about self-directed investors, people who like a little guidance, and people who give the adviser full discretion. Those segmentations break down when it comes to retirement assets. A $800,000 rollover probably presents you with the single largest financial decision you've made since you bought your first house. [With smaller amounts], you might have gone online and done a little asset allocation on your own. But it's much more challenging to make that decision for $800,000. Now you want advice in a way you didn't before."

Multiply that decision by the number of baby boomers now entering their sixties—America's largest-ever "retirement class"—and you have a huge and ongoing opportunity for independent advisers.

from "planner" to "investment adviser"

By the time the U.S. economy finally began to recover, in 1982, the mutual fund industry had matured considerably. Yet public acceptance hadn't quite kept pace; some investors still weren't ready to switch from the individual stocks they'd traditionally preferred. "We take it as a given now," says Kurt Cerulli, "but in the early 1980s, the mutual fund wasn't really front and center. People were buying individual stocks. It was the traditional 'get an idea from your broker and buy it' approach. It was all transaction-based and all commission-based."

Many financial planners continued to stick to fee-only planning and let clients arrange their own investments. Gradually, though, they began to realize that it made sense to offer investment advice as well as planning. As a business proposition, financial planning on its own was not very profitable. But when it was coupled with investment advice, for which ongoing fees could be charged based on the amount of assets under management, it suddenly became more attractive. A 1 percent fee applied to a client with a $1 million account, for example, would generate $10,000 in annual revenue, enough to cover the cost of planning and advisory services for the client and contribute to overhead and profit. One hundred such clients could make for a financially viable advisory practice.

Mutual funds became the investment vehicle of choice for several reasons. For one, funds were highly regulated. They were also relatively transparent—for example, funds are obliged to disclose their holdings twice a year—and straightforward to analyze. Diversification, low cost, and liquidity gave them an advantage over individual stocks and partnership interests. "Mutual funds played beautifully in the independent registered investment adviser market in many ways," says Cerulli. "A lot of the advisers throughout the 1980s were mutual fund asset allocators. They were able to put together diversified portfolios as the mutual fund vehicle became embraced as a mainstream product. The rise of equity investing and the general concept of diversified portfolios converged to make mutual funds attractive."

Fee-based planner-advisers tended not to promote a particular product—or any product at all, except advice. Their primary offering was objectivity. These planner-advisers "had no reason to choose one fund company or one fund provider over another," Cerulli says. "And there was no reason to buy and sell funds to generate a commission. Their compensation was based on managing a portfolio of mutual funds. So their interests were more aligned with their clients'."

Independent advisers using this model had to become skilled in analyzing and comparing mutual funds and their managers. As the number of funds grew from five hundred to more than three thousand during the 1980s, more and more advisers turned to a single resource for guidance: the mutual fund data service Morningstar.

"Their compensation was based on managing a portfolio of mutual funds. So their interests were more aligned with their clients."

—KURT CERULLI,
CERULLI ASSOCIATES

Two men were responsible for creating and shaping the world's first mutual fund data service: Joe Mansueto and Don Phillips. Mansueto, a securities analyst, founded Morningstar in 1984 in his Chicago apartment to fill a gap he'd observed between the growing interest in mutual funds and the amount of information available to individual investors. Later that year he published the firm's first product, the quarterly *Mutual Fund Sourcebook*. Don Phillips, who had earned a master's degree in American literature, joined the firm two years later as its first mutual fund analyst and, soon afterward, became the editor of its flagship publication, *Morningstar Mutual Funds*, a comprehensive guide to more than seven hundred funds. It quickly became the firm's most popular product.

"When Morningstar started we had no clue about the financial planning world," says Phillips. "We were just thinking like investors. We liked to invest in funds. What's the information we would want to know? We had no idea that this revolution was going on in financial planning—moving from selling products to finding the best possible investments for their clients.

"It turned out we had the exact same mindset as independent advisers did. We wanted to look objectively at where to put money. And that was the way they were thinking. This audience really found us. We didn't go out and target it. And it was a perfect fit."

> "We had no clue about the financial planning world. . . . We were just thinking like investors."

Throughout its history, Morningstar has continued to develop innovative information resources. Morningstar Principia, introduced in 1991, was one of the first software programs that financial advisers could use to analyze stock funds. Morningstar.com, the first of the company's Internet platforms, contains information and research on stocks, mutual funds, ETFs, hedge funds, and 529 college savings plans. Between 1998 and 2001, the company embarked on an overseas expansion to Japan, Australia, New Zealand, and Canada.

Today Morningstar serves more than 4.9 million investors and 185,000 financial advisers around the world.

In 1984, Morningstar published its first product, the quarterly *Mutual Fund Sourcebook*™ with performance data, portfolio holdings, and other information on approximately 400 mutual funds. In 1991, Morningstar introduced CD-ROM-based Principia software to help advisers analyze stock funds

"Advisers weren't necessarily experts on individual stocks," recalls Morningstar managing director Don Phillips, "but as the world moved from stocks to mutual funds, they felt they were equal to the challenge of identifying, selecting, and monitoring good mutual fund managers."

Morningstar was founded in 1984 to give individual investors useful information about mutual funds, but it wasn't long before financial planners and independent advisers became Morningstar's largest market. They remain so today. Many advisers believe that Morningstar's powerful tools played a key role in the growth and success of the independent advisory industry.

"If you're a little boutique or sole proprietor adviser, there's no way you can research stocks and bonds independently," says Peggy Ruhlin. "You've got to be working for a [large firm] or another institution that can do that research for you. Mutual funds gave a different approach to the game, but there was still the problem of research. Morningstar came along and solved that, giving us the tools to do our own research. We didn't have to be associated with a big broker-dealer—we now had the tools to do it on our own."

FIVE

An Industry Comes of Age

WITHIN WEEKS OF his inauguration in 1981, President Ronald Reagan declared that the United States was in "the worst economic mess since the Great Depression."[1] He quickly set about implementing policies he believed would turn the tide—chiefly tax cuts, a reduction of federal regulations, spending restraints, and a stable monetary policy. Known collectively, and sometimes derisively, as "Reagonomics," these policies were at least partly responsible for the dramatic change in the U.S. economic picture during the 1980s and 1990s. (In fact, some of the monetary policy changes had been initiated at the end of the Carter administration.) The economic malaise of the 1970s evaporated, inflation and interest rates dropped sharply, and the financial markets responded enthusiastically to Reagan's leadership. From their low point in August 1982, when the Dow Jones Industrial Average closed at 776.92, the markets began a vigorous and historic rally that lasted until 2000—the longest bull market in American history.

Not coincidentally, the 1980s and 1990s were also the decades when the largest demographic cohort in American history—the post–World War II baby boom generation—entered its prime earning years. Accustomed virtually since birth to being the center of media and marketplace attention, boomers approached investing with their

Boomer-generation investors turned in growing numbers to independent advisers

characteristic blend of skepticism and self-assurance. "The boomers are uncompromising," observes Dan Leemon, Charles Schwab & Co.'s former chief strategy officer. "They think they could do anything if they only had the time, and they won't compromise between advice and control as much of the industry—from the discount brokers to the full-commission guys—has required them to do."

The two booms—economic and demographic—powered an unprecedented expansion in market participation. And more than any other stimulus to date, they propelled the striking growth of the independent registered investment adviser industry. Suddenly, there seemed to be a dizzying array of investment products from which to choose: not only the increasingly popular money market mutual funds, which had been introduced in the early 1970s, but also bond funds, equity funds, and the exciting new technology stocks. Investors who had first ventured into the markets in the 1970s, when banks were paying 5 percent interest and money market funds were paying double-digit rates, were now migrating to longer-term investments such as bond and stock funds, whose returns now outpaced those of the shorter-term money market funds. And boomer investors—whose self-image included the concept of "independent spirit"—were less likely than their elders had been to seek out traditional sources of investment advice. Instead, they turned in growing numbers to independent advisers, in whom they found the ideal combination of advice, comprehensive reporting, transparent pricing, and a sense of control in the form of performance measurement.

By 1983, the stage was set for independent advisers to play a significantly more important role in the industry. To make that happen, the profession would need accessible technology, a centralized exchange for no-load mutual funds, and a new approach to financial planning. Within just a few years, all three needs would be met.

the technology solution

The first *deus ex machina* to come to the rescue was literally a machine: the IBM Personal Computer. Until its advent, independent advisers—who hadn't been able to afford the expensive mainframe computers used by large financial institutions—had been awash in paper. Infor-

mation from clients, brokers, and custodians came into the office on paper forms and was processed by hand, transferred to other paper forms, and later consolidated and reconciled by hand. Many independent advisers had put their clients' investments into no-load mutual funds; lacking an electronic clearinghouse, they had to plow through paperwork required by individual fund companies every time shares in the fund were bought or sold. The work was slow and laborious—and it severely limited the number of clients an independent firm could serve.

The IBM PC, introduced in 1981, and its ever-more-powerful successors changed all that. The PC made quick work of portfolio accounting. Gradually, many advisory firms automated many of their primary functions, from financial planning to customer relationship management to asset allocation and account rebalancing.

One of those firms was Fisher Investments of Woodside, California, which manages assets for institutions and affluent individuals. Kenneth L. Fisher—who is also known as a *Forbes* columnist and the author of four books about finance—founded the firm in 1979 as a small independent shop. "When PCs emerged with rudimentary hard-disk drives," Fisher recalls, "you could see the potential to do things that before only a bigger firm could have done, and to provide a new level of professionalism. Before then it had been very hard for a little firm to grow—it was way too labor intensive and too hard to have a high degree of accuracy. The PC allowed us to think big. I remember sitting down with my wife and showing her on a marker board how I could eventually have $100 million under management. That seemed like a heck of a lot of money. That would be pretty good thing." As of March 2007, Fisher Investments has more than $37 billion in assets under management.

Although the IBM PC was not the first personal computer to run spreadsheet programs (the earlier Apple II and the Osborn had had their own versions), it popularized them among advisers. Spreadsheets automated the tedious item-by-item hand-calculations advisers had performed when they did financial projections for their clients. Joel Bruckenstein, a consultant on adviser technology issues and the publisher of *Virtual Office News*, an industry newsletter, recalls that "before commercial financial planning software existed, advisers simply designed their own spreadsheets." As the programs evolved, from VisiCalc to SuperCalc to Lotus 1-2-3 and eventually to Microsoft Excel, their capabilities and computing power grew exponentially.

But one critical task—portfolio accounting, which tracks which clients own which securities in which accounts—was not efficient for do-it-yourself spreadsheets. Indeed, portfolio accounting had for decades vexed independent advisers, especially those with individual clients. In many instances, a client household would have a portfolio of investment accounts—regular taxable accounts as well as tax-deferred retirement plans, IRAs, and annuities. There could also be trusts and custodial or college accounts for children and grandchildren. Before computers, advisers tracked this portfolio of accounts with manual entries in ledgers—or, by the 1960s, on three-by-five-inch index cards. It was far from a perfect solution. For one thing, the banks and broker-dealers that held client assets in custody provided only basic information. "All you typically got from a custodian was a statement of account, with your holdings and current values," says Bruckenstein. "They didn't track performance, cash flows, or the cost basis of your holdings for tax purposes. To do any of that you needed portfolio-management software."

Now, with the PC gaining acceptance, that software began to materialize. Early offerings of portfolio-management programs running on the PC's disk operating system included dbCAMS and Captools, and Advent's Professional Portfolio. In 1983, Stephanie DiMarco founded Advent Software in San Francisco, and the firm's Professional Portfolio product became the first portfolio-management software built specifically for the PC. A decade later in 1993, Advent redeveloped its core product for the Microsoft Windows operating system, branded it Axys, and it subsequently became the industry leader. Eventually, portfolio-management systems became ubiquitous among independent advisers. In its 2006 study of advisory firms, the consulting firm Moss Adams found that portfolio reporting was the least likely of major advisory firm functions still to be performed manually.

Veteran independent advisers like Rick Keller, president of The Keller Group Investment Management of Irvine, California, remember the dramatic impact portfolio-management systems had on their businesses. "We brought in Advent's original portfolio management solution, and that changed everything," Keller says. "We were able to produce client statements in a more timely manner. And when a client came in, instead of having to get on the telephone and call all the fund companies to give me the value of the client's accounts, I'd have it that morning from the previous day's close. It saved us a couple people, which was huge. I could have those people focus on value-added services instead of mundane bookkeeping chores."

Advent's portfolio management products, Professional Portfolio and Axys®, dramatically improved advisers' efficiency in managing investments

The Pivotal Advantage in Portfolio Management

Using Axys

Axys™

ADVENT

INTRODUCING THE PROFESSIONAL PORTFOLIO

How advisory firm functions are performed

	Packaged software	Custom software	Manually performed	Outsourced/ automated
Portfolio reporting	56%	10%	10%	24%
Financial planning	59	19	19	3
Account aggregation	47	12	19	22
Accounts payable/ receivable	56	8	27	9
Client relationship management	57	10	32	1
Data storage/document management	37	14	33	17
Trade confirmation processing	26	6	34	34
Asset allocation	35	24	35	5
Investment policy/ proposal generation	23	28	43	6
Account processing and rebalancing	26	15	45	14
Alternative investment planning models	11	16	58	14
Compliance	9	7	59	25
License and registration management	6	4	69	21

SOURCE: *Financial Performance Study of Advisory Firms*, Moss Adams (Seattle: 2006), 46.

NOTE: Rows have been re-ranked in ascending order of "manually performed" ranking.

simulation, diversification, and optimization

Beyond simply keeping track of clients' investments, PC technology allowed advisers to bring a much greater degree of sophistication to their financial planning services and private-client investment advice. For the first time, they had the computing power to make complex calculations about asset allocation and portfolio diversification. Advisers could also simulate scenarios and project outcomes—all without leaving their desks.

It wasn't the theories that were new, only the tools. Modern portfolio theory, for example, had been developed in the early 1950s as a way to quantify the "don't put all your eggs in one basket" axiom. Portfolio-management theory showed how to measure the risks of various securities and combine them to produce optimal returns for an investor's level of risk tolerance, based on theoretical models. But it wasn't until the early 1990s that computer programs known as mean-variance optimizers brought portfolio theory within the reach of independent advisers. By the end of the decade, the software was advanced enough to generate recommendations based on specific client goals and circumstances.

During the early 1990s advisers gained a second powerful tool: Monte Carlo simulations. This statistical technique, first used during World War II when the atomic bomb was being developed, helps forecast the range and probability of future uncertain outcomes. The complexity of Monte Carlo models and the need to repeat the simulations thousands of times require substantial computer power, which by the 1990s was finally available on desktop PCs. Independent advisers could use Monte Carlo models to estimate the probability that a client would run out of money during retirement, taking into account the client's age, life expectancy, current assets, spending rate, inflation, and the expected returns and risks of various investments.

Technology advances enabled advisers to do more than just serve clients more effectively. They also transformed businesses. The number of clients a small firm could serve grew by an order of magnitude, and advisers turned their attention to building their businesses.

Mathematician Stanislaw Ulam helped develop the Monte Carlo Method while working on the Manhattan Project. Today, advisers use Monte Carlo models to forecast the range and probability of future uncertain outcomes

HARRY MARKOWITZ: PIONEER OF MODERN PORTFOLIO THEORY

In 1952, Harry Markowitz, a 25-year-old economist with the RAND Corporation, published an article called "Portfolio Selection" that examined the effects of risk and diversification on portfolio returns. The article became the cornerstone of modern portfolio theory (MPT), which says that portfolio diversification reduces risk and enhances expected return over time—a concept that seems obvious today but was revolutionary when Markowitz introduced it.

Markowitz had never intended to become an economist. Growing up in Chicago, the son of grocery-store owners, he enjoyed reading popular physics and astronomy. In high school he read Charles Darwin's *The Origin of Species*, which impressed him with its "marshaling of facts and careful consideration of possible objections," as he later put it. He also began reading the works of serious philosophers, including David Hume, who observed that "though we release a ball a thousand times, and each time, it falls to the floor, we do not have a

> **Diversification reduces risk—the concept seems obvious today but was revolutionary when Markowitz introduced it.**

necessary proof that it will fall the thousand-and-first time."

During his first two years at the University of Chicago, Markowitz studied philosophy. He settled on economics only as an upper-division student. His instructors included four giants in the field, all of whom influenced him greatly: Milton Friedman, Jacob Marschak, L. J. Savage, and Tjalling Koopmans.

Markowitz later wrote that the basic concepts of portfolio theory came to him one afternoon in the library while he was reading John Burr Williams's *Theory of Investment Value*, which proposed that the value of a stock should equal the present value of its future dividends. "But if the investor were only interested in expected values of securities," Markowitz wrote, "he or she would only be interested in the expected value of the portfolio; and to maximize the expected value of a portfolio one need invest only in a single security. This, I knew, was not the way investors did or should act. Investors diversify because they

In 1990, U.S. economists Harry Markowitz (above), William F. Sharpe, and Merton H. Miller shared the Nobel Prize for their contributions to financial economics. Markowitz is best known for his pioneering work in modern portfolio theory

are concerned with risk as well as return. Variance came to mind as a measure of risk. The fact that portfolio variance depended on security covariances added to the plausibility of the approach. Since there were two criteria, risk and return, it was natural to assume that investors selected from the set of Pareto optimal risk-return combinations." [2]

In 1990, Markowitz and two colleagues were awarded the Nobel Prize in economics for their work in this area. Today, portfolio managers everywhere routinely use techniques based on Markowitz's insights.

the clearinghouse solution

Mutual funds had first gained modest popularity in the 1960s, during the last big bull market. Money market mutual funds, introduced a decade later, proved especially popular among investors and independent advisers alike, especially as yields rose in the early 1980s. Individual investors found no-load funds—which charged no commission on transactions—especially appealing, because all their money could go to work for them. But if they invested in more than one no-load fund, things got complicated. Investors in funds from six no-load companies, for example, had six phone numbers to call and six sets of statements to manage.

Brokerage firm Charles Schwab & Co., Inc., which served do-it-yourself investors, saw the problem as an opportunity. In 1984 Schwab launched the Mutual Fund Marketplace® to give investors a convenient place to buy and sell no-load funds from multiple fund companies. Customers received a single statement and a centralized platform with access to 140 no-load funds. (By 2007, the funds and fund families numbered in the thousands.) In exchange for the convenience, customers were asked to pay a small transaction fee for each trade, even though no-load funds could be purchased directly from each sponsoring fund company.

At first, Schwab did not aggressively promote the Mutual Fund Marketplace. The company advertised the service only through small weekly ads in an inside section of the *Wall Street Journal*. "We had mixed feelings," recalled John McGonigle, a Schwab senior vice president who in the mid-1980s was head of the firm's mutual fund business. "Because we were a discount broker, it was awkward for us to also be the world's most expensive place to buy no-load funds. So most of our clients didn't know we offered that service."

Do-it-yourself customers may have been slow to learn about Mutual Fund Marketplace, and reluctant to pay the transaction fee when they did learn about it, but independent advisers—in particular, those who charged fees rather than commissions—quickly grasped its advantages. Even more than individual investors, they were hampered by the lack of a centralized exchange through which to purchase no-load funds. "We were managing no-load mutual funds, but the assets were custodied at the individual fund companies," says David H. Bugen of Regent Atlantic Capital, an independent advisory firm in Chatham, New Jersey. It was very cumbersome to reduce the allocation in one fund or stop using a fund and move to another fund group. First we had to get signature guarantees, then the check would go back to the client, and then the client would have to fill out another application."

Not surprisingly, some fee-only financial planning firms in effect threw up their hands; they limited their work to planning and didn't offer advice about security selection. "We used to tell clients, 'You need to invest the money in mutual funds, stocks and bonds, and other products," says Peggy Ruhlin, of Budros Ruhlin & Roe, an independent registered investment adviser in Columbus, Ohio. "Then we'd say, 'So, do you know any brokers? Why don't you go to one of them?' And clients would ask us, 'Why don't you guys do it?' Well, we didn't have the tools." When the firm finally agreed to help clients with investments, it had them open accounts with a number of no-load mutual funds, Ruhlin says. "They'd get statements from this fund company, that company, all the other ones. We would receive copies as well."

The paperwork burden was overwhelming. "We had only about ten clients," says Mary A. Malgoire, president of The Family Firm in Bethesda, Maryland. "But the volume of paperwork was so heavy that we couldn't deal with growing the business." Malgoire was an early president of the National Association of Personal Financial Advisors, whose members are fee-only financial planners. "I had what I thought was a great idea at the time," she recalls. "We had five or six no-load fund exhibitors at one conference. I got them all in a meeting and said, 'If you could create an organization that would allow automatic transfers between your fund families for our clients, that would be so helpful. We would put our clients' money there and all the different funds would be available. That would just break this whole thing wide open.' And they all looked at each other and they said, 'Well, I don't want to be doing anything with other fund companies.'"

Malgoire's idea for automated transactions among no-load fund families was, in fact, what Schwab offered with its Mutual Fund

Marketplace—an innovation now seen as a watershed in the history of independent advisers. "Prior to the 1980s there weren't any ways for investment advisers to deal with a handful of mutual fund companies," says Kurt Cerulli, president of the financial-services research firm Cerulli Associates. It was the emergence of the service-agent platform, initially from Schwab, that enabled them to grow."

It worked like this: An adviser would instruct his or her clients to open brokerage accounts and transfer their investment assets to Schwab. The adviser would obtain legal authorization from each client in the form of a limited power of attorney allowing the adviser to make buy and sell transactions in the account. Advisers could manage the accounts with phone calls to Schwab. It was a huge advance, says David Bugen of Regent Atlantic Capital: "The consolidation with a centralized custodian enabled advisers and their staffs to become more efficient and more effective, and to spend more time on client issues as opposed to paperwork."

Interestingly, Schwab had not promoted Mutual Fund Marketplace among independent advisers. In fact, Schwab had had very little awareness of the advisers' very existence. The company discovered that some advisers were availing themselves of the new Mutual Fund Marketplace only after it conducted a review of accounts with limited powers of attorney. All of a sudden, advisers began to look like a very real business opportunity. After all, each adviser represented much more than a single new customer bringing one household's investment assets to Schwab. Rather, an adviser might bring the assets of fifty or a hundred households—often wealthy ones. The idea of providing custody, trading, and related services to these advisers began to seem very attractive. Even more attractive was the fact that no major competitors had an eye on the business.

"We saw an expansion in the number of startup investment advisers—firms with $10 million to $50 million," says Jim Hackley, a former Schwab senior vice president closely involved with the launch of the company's adviser business. "These shops were too small to interest an institutional custody provider. Nobody other than Schwab seemed to want their business, much less seek it out. For the most part we serendipitously jumped on a wave as it was surging."

On "Black Monday"—
October 19, 1987—the
Dow Jones Industrial
Average (DJIA) lost
22.61% of its value in a
single day

Actually, it wasn't quite that simple. Schwab's computer systems were set up for individual customers. They could not recognize or handle groups of customers that needed to be aggregated for trading and recordkeeping purposes. It took more than two years, and a substantial financial investment, to develop the kind of accounting, known as master/sub, that could accomplish this task. By this time, PCs for data communications were well established, and Schwab began work on SchwabLink®, a system enabling daily downloads of client account information directly into the PCs and portfolio-management programs of independent advisers.

In 1985, Schwab opened its custody business for advisers, originally known as Financial Advisors Service; the formal launch was in 1987. (In 1993, the business was renamed Schwab Institutional® to better reflect the services offered to investment managers.) It owed its success to service, technology, and Schwab's willingness to listen to and learn from advisers looking for a better way to buy mutual funds. "In the beginning, we didn't know anything at all about their business," admits John Philip Coghlan, a former president of Schwab Institutional. "So we sat down with advisers and asked questions about the problems in their business. We'd hear, 'I'm drowning in a sea of paper as I grow my business. I can't even add people fast enough, nor can I pay them to keep up with this exponential avalanche of paperwork and forms that I'm creating.' By being completely ignorant about a potential new business that was right there in front of us, we created an entirely new approach to the business. It was all about asking questions—and listening to the answers." One thing Coghlan and his Schwab colleagues discovered was that "once a quarter many advisers had to shut down their offices for three days to a week to send invoices to their clients. And every quarter clients had an opportunity to say, 'I don't know, this quarter I just really don't feel like writing this check. The performance wasn't as good as I've seen in the past.'" To address this problem, Schwab developed client-authorized direct debiting of advisers' fees from client accounts. "Once we learned about the problem, we were able to move quickly to fix it," says Coghlan.

Mary Malgoire remembers the pace at which Schwab rolled out enhancements to its new adviser platform. "I was one of the first members of the Schwab advisory board," she says. "It was an interesting experience because they were really tapping us: 'What do you guys want? We'll put it together. We'll make it happen.' We said, 'We want more funds. We want transfers to go faster. We want to be able to buy a bond.' Schwab was picking our brains and then moving on it. And they moved fast."

The industry began to change perceptibly as leading independent

In 1991, SchwabLink (formerly Account AccessLink) was launched, offering advisers expanded account and data management capabilities

SchwabLink™ User's Manual

SchwabLink

advisory firms adopted Schwab's platform. "Investment advisers in the mid-1980s started to get much more powerful thanks to the service-agent platforms," says Kurt Cerulli. "They stopped being a sleepy cottage industry and started to emerge as an alternative to large, established competitors."

In those early years, Schwab had the independent adviser business to itself. "Schwab was very much the Henry Ford of brokerage firms," says Coghlan. "You could have any color you wanted as long as it was black. Schwab had this single transaction-processing machine, and it did wonderfully on investments that could be run right through the machine. So stocks were fabulous through that machine, and later options. Mutual funds required a very different system, but Schwab made the necessary [technology] investment. But anything that didn't fit within the basic 'factory' model was more of a challenge. And advisers, because they were knowledgeable and because they had access to other investment opportunities, wanted Schwab to be able to handle those other assets. Schwab recognized that one of its strengths was this fabulous scale. And yet the adviser business required a customized approach that took the scale out of the system."

Mutual Fund OneSource: the key to growth

By 1992, when Schwab launched its next major innovation, Mutual Fund OneSource®, independent advisers were no longer a minor, overlooked constituency. On the contrary, they played an important role in the development and eventual success of Mutual Fund OneSource.

Mutual Fund OneSource had a straightforward yet radical mission: to offer no-load mutual funds without a transaction fee. The fund companies paid Schwab an asset-based fee for transaction, recordkeeping, and shareholder services it provided; customers paid no transaction fees. To entice "star" funds into the program, Schwab invited only the top twenty fund families as measured by Schwab client assets in the Mutual Fund Marketplace and gave them an exclusive contract.

Advisers welcomed the new service, and their enthusiasm

encouraged more no-load fund companies, which initially had been reluctant, to participate. "When we first approached the no-load fund companies and said, 'Look, if you pay us so we can eliminate the transaction fee, we'll do a lot more business,' they were luke-warm," says John McGonigle. They asked us, 'Why should we pay you to get between us and the customers?' But they also saw that the adviser business was beginning to grow and become more important. Through Mutual Fund OneSource, they had a way to appeal to advisers. And so they said, 'OK, we'll sign up.' It's clear to me that Mutual Fund OneSource never would have happened had we not already had the independent adviser service."

One no-load fund executive who was quick to spot the advantages of Mutual Fund OneSource was Peter Sundman, now president of Neuberger Berman Funds. Still, he admits that the concept "was a very tough pill to swallow" at first.

"I remember vividly the day [the Schwab team] came into our offices and said, 'All right, tonight's your final shot,'" Sundman says. "'We've got five [fund] companies and we're going to go live with them.' My boss didn't think we could take that kind of a hit to revenue. He politely kicked the guy from Schwab out of his office. I got our CFO and a few other senior people from Neuberger and started arguing. I said if it was a 50 percent cut to our revenue, 50 percent on a much bigger number still meant a lot of revenue. And that if we didn't do this, we were going to be left on the sidelines.

"I could clearly see from my dealings with financial advisers that Mutual Fund OneSource was going to change the world. And in the end we called the guy from Schwab in his hotel room and signed on as the sixth fund company in that original grouping.

"My boss had said, 'All right, big shot, what do you think the number is?' I said, 'If they're successful, we could raise several hundred million dollars on the platform.' Little did I know that in three years we'd have billions."

As fund companies signed up for the no-transaction fee program, independent advisers stood in the middle of a virtuous circle of accelerating growth. "All of a sudden our offering to advisers, and therefore their offering to *their* clients, became more powerful and more appealing, and so they grew," says McGonigle. "That

Charles Schwab

___

Mutual Fund
OneSource
Service

Now you can invest
in over 250
mutual funds –
with no loads and
no transaction fees.

___

Independent
advisers played
an important role
in the eventual
success of Mutual
Fund OneSource

growth benefited us as well as the fund companies that had signed up early. So more fund companies wanted to sign up, and the next thing we knew we had a thousand funds in Mutual Fund OneSource."

At that time three lines of business accessed the Mutual Fund Marketplace and Mutual Fund OneSource: retail, 401(k), and advisers. "Advisers were my most important clients," says McGonigle. "I spent as much time as I could with them understanding their needs and wants. I paid some attention to retail and some attention to 401(k), but I focused on advisers, because they were doing this full time. They were students of the game. They knew what they wanted and they were at the leading edge. If I could evolve the Mutual Fund Marketplace to meet their needs, two years later I would have what retail needed, and the next year I'd have what 401(k) needed. So I was really focused on helping those advisers."

Before long, other providers took note of Schwab's success and looked for ways to emulate it. Among the firms that introduced custody offerings for independent advisers in the 1990s were Jack White & Co., Waterhouse Securities, and Fidelity Investments. "Whether through market research or from observing Schwab, Fidelity had a strategic intent to get into the adviser business," says Jay Lanigan, former president of Fidelity Registered Investment Advisor Group, who had been with the firm since 1980 and joined its investment adviser group in 1993, a year after Fidelity launched its advisory business. "We'd started it as part of our retail brokerage business, but by 1993 we decided to focus on our adviser business as part of our institutional business. At that time, we had $400 million in custodied assets for advisers—really quite small. By the time I left the company, at the beginning of 2005, that figure had grown to $140 billion. It's now well over $200 billion."

Lanigan and others in the industry agree that technology has been a key component of the custodial business. "The custodians in this industry are continuing to come out with better and better technology," says Tom Bradley, president of TD Ameritrade Institutional, the successor organization to the adviser businesses at Jack White and Waterhouse. "All our platforms are living entities. We're constantly making enhancements to them. What started as an interface to some portfolio-management systems has blossomed into full-blown platforms that enable advisory firms to run incredibly efficient and effective businesses."

financial planning and
money management join forces

The third dramatic change in the independent adviser industry occurred among firms offering financial planning. Though the number of financial planners grew rapidly in the 1980s, financial planning itself was not turning out to be a highly remunerative profession. Planners typically charged fees for what amounted to very technical, labor-intensive work gathering large amounts of information about their clients' finances, analyzing it, and preparing detailed recommendations. Financial plans tended to be one-time-only sales; the client was unlikely to purchase a second plan. And while in a perfect world planning would be an ongoing process, many clients were unwilling to pay a retainer fee for continuing advice. "As financial planners, our earnings were limited by the number of plans we could do," recalls Elaine Bedel, president of Bedel Financial Consulting, an independent advisory firm in Indianapolis. "You could build a firm if you kept leveraging yourself, but you were still limited."

Of the 7,000 financial planners registered as investment advisers in 1987, only 2,100 said they provided money-management services, according to a 1988 Securities and Exchange Commission report. "A financial planner usually does not manage client assets," the study reported. "Instead, the planner's primary service is to prepare a financial plan for the client, and to offer advice as to the purchase or sale of specific financial products appropriate to the implementation of the plan."[3]

Financial planners generally fell into two broad business types: those working on a commission basis and those who were fee-only planners. Commissioned planners typically operated as representatives of independent broker-dealers. Sometimes they also had their own registered investment advisory firms while offering commissioned products through their broker-dealer affiliates. Fee-only planners, in contrast, did not accept commissions and operated solely as independent registered investment advisers. They generally implemented their plans with no-load products. As the SEC report noted, "With some financial planners the process ends with the presentation of a financial plan, for which the planner is

MONETA GROUP INVESTMENT ADVISORS: EVOLUTION OF AN INDUSTRY LEADER

Peter Schick

Like many other advisory firms, Moneta Group Investment Advisors of St. Louis, Missouri, began life as something else entirely—in this case, a company handling employee benefits, insurance business, and planning for physicians. Its evolution into a large independent investment advisory and financial planning firm is the history in microcosm of the investment adviser industry.

The story begins in 1974, when Peter Schick left the Air Force and joined his father at the firm in St. Louis. Schick's approach, popular at the time, was called needs-based selling, a precursor to financial planning in which the salesman prepares a profile of the client and calculates the appropriate amount. "The problem," said Moneta Group president Joe Sheehan, "was they couldn't get over thinking that once a sale was made, they were done. In fact, financial planning has to be an ongoing process."

The seeds of transformation were planted in the early 1980s, when Schick heard a presentation about a multidiscipline financial planning practice and decided to implement the concept at Moneta. By 1986 the firm had added CPAs, an attorney, and a trust officer to its staff and was doing comprehensive financial planning.

Moneta Group's second big change occurred after one of its new CPAs, Jay Ring, attended a Chartered Financial Planning conference. He proposed to Schick that Moneta start charging fees for advice—which meant the firm would have to become a registered investment adviser. It took some persuading, but in the end Schick paid what Sheehan calls "the whopping sum of $15,000" to form a registered investment adviser, Moneta Group Investment Advisors. *Moneta* is the Latin word for a mint in which coins are made.

The notion that clients would pay for advice wasn't an easy sell, Sheehan says. Some principals left the firm. In response, "Peter began recruiting people who were more interested in providing advice and long-term finan-cial planning and less inter-ested in transaction selling," said Sheehan.

"In the very early days we would put half the client's money in commissioned products and half into non-commissioned products, charging a fee on the non-commissioned products," Sheehan recalled. "It was a challenge: the no-load funds didn't recognize us, and we had

> **The evolution of Moneta Group … is the history in microcosm of the investment adviser industry.**

no central custodian, since our broker-dealer would not hold no-load funds."

One of the Moneta principals went to a Schwab convention and discovered that Schwab would act as custodian for the firm's no-load business. "Next we learned about Axys, the portfolio-management system from Advent," Sheehan said. "Those two advances allowed us to expand our ability to provide service, information, and advice." Although slow to take effect, the change was dramatic. "Productivity went through the roof," Sheehan said. "All of a sudden, all those investment issues became scalable."

In the mid-1990s Moneta Group's revenue was 85 per-cent from commissions and 15 percent from fees, says Sheehan. "Today it's 100 percent fees. And we have $6.2 billion in assets [as of April 2007]. The reinvention of Moneta Group turned out to be a pretty good deal."

compensated by a fee. In the more typical situation, however, once the client is presented with the plan, the implementation of the plan includes the purchase of investment or insurance products specifically recommended by the planner. Thus the planner may be affiliated with a broker-dealer, or with an insurance company, or both. And the planner's remuneration for the client may come more from commissions on the sale of products than from fees generated by the presentation of the plan."[4]

Indeed, implementation was the way most financial planners were able to stay in business. According to Dr. William Anthes, president of the College for Financial Planning during the 1980s, "If you can combine the planning process with implementation of that process, the chances of your being more successful are going to be much higher. It's a lot easier for an individual or firm to be viable if they can link the planning process with the step that involves implementation."

Before the spread of back-office technology at independent firms, implementation for most financial planners meant having a broker-dealer affiliation and a commission-based business model. Broker-dealers provided support and investment products to their independent commissioned planner representatives, while fee-only advisers were on their own. As a result, most financial planners at the time worked on commission. "Being a fee-only financial planner was very rare," recalls Bedel. "When I first opened my own shop, people around the country told me, 'You're a fool, Elaine. You're leaving all this money on the table [by not taking commissions].' And they probably were right, but it just wasn't comfortable for me. I came through a fee-only route to doing financial planning, where many others came from the insurance industry or the brokerage industry, and charging commissions was just part of what they did."

Then came desktop computing, and with it a transformation of the financial planning business. Thanks to computers, commission-based planners no longer needed the support of their broker-dealer affiliates and could operate solely as investment advisers. This freed them to base their businesses on asset-based fees and enabled them to become truly independent in terms of their operations and the products they recommended for clients. Sometimes, this transition would take a number of years, as it did for Moneta Group Investment Advisors of St. Louis, Missouri. (See the company history on page 94.) But the effort was widely seen to be worthwhile.

As independent advisory businesses became more viable, brokers at large full-service firms began migrating to it. The trend began slowly but grew steadily throughout the 1990s and early 2000s.

The back-office capabilities inherent in desktop computing had another beneficial effect: they made it possible to combine financial planning and money management profitably under the same roof. Asset-based fees from money management services supported ongoing financial planning and made possible a level of profitability that assured success. "People with financial planning backgrounds had been charging, say, $2,000, to develop a financial plan for a client—a book that then sat on the client's shelf," says former Schwab Institutional president Coghlan. "Clients began to realize that they wanted help in implementing the plan's recommendations. And advisers, in turn, asked themselves: 'Do I want to sell a $2,000 book to one client and then look for somebody else to sell to? Or would I rather take care of the first client's bigger investing problem and be paid on a regular basis as the assets grow?'"

Handling investments enabled firms to expand their range of offerings. Financial planners who catered to wealthy customers came to be known as wealth managers, offering services such as estate planning, tax planning and preparation, asset-protection planning, sophisticated investment strategies, advice to business owners, assistance to clients in philanthropic activities, and even family office services such as property management and travel planning. Firms that started as small planning shops eventually found themselves topping the $1 billion mark in assets under management.

No single factor accounts for the remarkable recent growth of independent advisers, notes Peter Sundman of Neuberger Berman Funds. "The Schwab platform enabled financial planners to take it to that next step and implement for clients," he points out. "But more significant in the end was the fact that advisers could get paid a percentage of the assets rather than an hourly or flat fee. That's what made the industry really take off."

SEPTEMBER
17
MONDAY

SIX

At the Crossroads

FIRST, DEVASTATION. Then—silence.

The trading floor of the New York Stock Exchange, usually frenzied on a weekday morning, was empty and echoing.

The computers at NASDAQ, which had glowed nonstop during the recent dot-com boom and collapse, were dark.

The bond markets stopped trading. The telephones of stockbrokers, investment bankers, and financial advisers stopped ringing.

On the morning of September 11, 2001, as the twin towers of the World Trade Center burned and collapsed, shock waves reverberated from lower Manhattan to the rest of the country—and the world. Just blocks from Ground Zero, Wall Street virtually shut down, crippled by damage to communication systems and stunned by the loss of hundreds of financial services employees whose offices were destroyed in the attacks.

The stock and bond markets opened briefly that Tuesday morning, then closed. The New York Stock Exchange remained shuttered for three more business days—only the third time in history it had been closed for so long, and the first time since 1933. When Wall Street did return to work, the stock indices betrayed the nation's fear and concern, closing sharply down.

Enron came to symbolize corporate fraud and corruption; its fall further eroded investor confidence

For anyone working in the financial markets—or investing in them—it was a dark and anxious time. Patriotic displays and the Bush administration's quick military response in Afghanistan helped rally spirits, but investors, already sobered by the bear market that had begun in 2000, remained wary.

Economic recovery was slow and incremental, hampered by ongoing concerns about terrorism and the challenges of military involvements in Iraq and Afghanistan. Investors in particular had reason to worry: in the early years of the new century Wall Street was still reeling from the collapse of the dot-com economy; the implosion of high-profile companies such as Enron, Tyco, and WorldCom; and the loss of several trillion dollars in stock values that followed. Beginning in 2002 the financial community faced a new challenge: a series of investigations, most notably by New York attorney general Eliot Spitzer, into the practices of mutual fund companies and investment banks. Hundreds of lawsuits were filed against securities houses whose analysts had allegedly misrepresented stocks during the bull market. There was political uncertainty as well, as President Bush's popularity dwindled from its post–9/11 high and the country prepared for a contentious 2004 national election.

In the end, corporations and investors proved surprisingly resilient. The wave of scandals, and the resulting legislation and regulation, forced companies to tighten their governance and increase their internal controls. Investors, toughened by recent experience, learned to adapt to more frequent bad news at home and abroad—changes in the terror "threat level," higher oil and gas prices, the 2004 Madrid bombing, the 2005 London transit attack, the December 2004 tsunami in Indonesia—without fleeing in panic. The stock markets began to turn around in October 2002, but it was not until after a new, steep downturn in March 2003 that a new bull market commenced in earnest.

Among those who helped guide the recovery's course were independent advisers, whose prudence and moderation had been a steadying force throughout the "new economy" mania of the late 1990s. A confluence of trends had propelled them to the forefront, making their profession one of the fastest-growing sectors in financial services. New business models, including the emergence of the wealth-management specialty, and new types of investments gave

New York Attorney
General Eliot Spitzer (left)
and New York Stock
Exchange Chairman
Richard Grasso discussing
a landmark stock-
research settlement

independent advisers greater flexibility in their services. The Internet—responsible for so many lost fortunes at the end of the twentieth century—turned into a tremendous boon for independent advisers and their clients. A huge population of baby boomers, now entering their fifties and sixties, brought their iconoclasm and skepticism into independent advisers' offices, seeking guidance from professionals who didn't fit into the "big business" mold. And as global markets continued to expand, the independent advisory profession found new markets around the world, in countries as disparate as China and Australia.

For a century that had begun in flames and fear, it was looking like a very promising era indeed.

growth and diversification

The most obvious indication of that promise was statistical. In 1999, according to research done by Cerulli Associates, 11,728 independent adviser firms were registered with the SEC or with state agencies. After several years of modest growth, the number shot up to 13,920 in 2003; by 2005 it had reached 15,540. "The independent advisory industry has quietly grown into a financial powerhouse over the last 25 years," observed the authors of a 2005 study conducted by

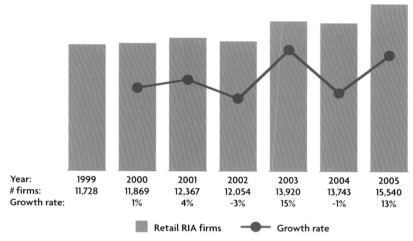

Number of registered investment adviser firms continues to grow

Year:	1999	2000	2001	2002	2003	2004	2005
# firms:	11,728	11,869	12,367	12,054	13,920	13,743	15,540
Growth rate:		1%	4%	-3%	15%	-1%	13%

◼ Retail RIA firms   ●— Growth rate

SOURCE: Cerulli Associates

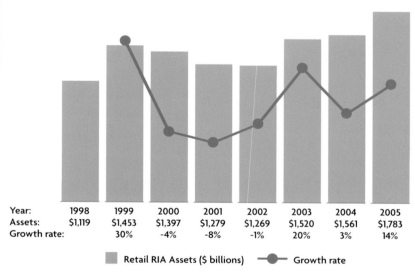

Retail registered investment adviser assets continue to grow

Year:	1998	1999	2000	2001	2002	2003	2004	2005
Assets:	$1,119	$1,453	$1,397	$1,279	$1,269	$1,520	$1,561	$1,783
Growth rate:		30%	-4%	-8%	-1%	20%	3%	14%

◼ Retail RIA Assets ($ billions)   ●— Growth rate

SOURCE: Cerulli Associates

J. P. Morgan Asset Management. "Driven by an exploding demand for non-conflicted, competent financial advice and further fueled in its earlier years by a roaring bull market, independent advisers today control over $1 trillion of assets."[1]

But numbers told only a small part of the story. Even more important to the industry's success has been a robust and innovative diversification in business models and offerings. Not only are there more types of advisory firms than ever before, in a greater variety of specializations, but—happily for the industry and its clients—all of them are flourishing.

The trend began in the late 1980s, when some independent advisers began combining financial planning and money management into a single service. Now other business models emerged. Some firms emphasized financial planning and delegated investments to outside money managers, others did the reverse. Some, in particular the new category of advisers known as wealth managers, developed and implemented financial plans, working directly with clients to select individual securities and funds and making referrals to outside experts as needed.

Other independent advisers have chosen to provide neither financial planning nor money management, operating instead as investment consultants. Like institutional pension consultants, they offer their affluent and sophisticated clients comprehensive investment-management services, including evaluating, selecting, and monitoring outside money managers. They may also offer estate and tax planning, assist clients in developing investment policy statements, and prepare asset-allocation plans.

Yet another type of independent adviser is the money manager who serves individual clients (and sometimes institutional clients such as pension funds and endowments). Some money managers apply specific portfolio strategies to all their clients—for example, investing for small-cap value or large-cap growth—while others create portfolios customized for each client's unique situation. The latter group includes firms that operate in the same manner as investment counselors, the original form of independent advisory firm that emerged in the 1920s. The direct relationship with the manager adds value, said Doug Lane, head of Douglas C. Lane & Associates in New York City:

> You're dealing directly with the people who are making the decisions on the stocks, doing the research, and handling your portfolio. People worth $1 million or $2 million get tired of mutual funds. They want to own a portfolio of individual stocks. They should have a direct relationship. We think it's an advantage if the people who are doing the research know the clients, because then they'll find better companies for them. And communications and performance will be better because of that direct relationship.

Increasingly, however, many independent advisers see themselves not as portfolio managers but rather as financial quarterbacks for their clients, coordinating services from a range of specialists who may include lawyers, accountants, and portfolio managers. This is the service-delivery model employed by advisers known as wealth managers. They are among the most successful of the independent advisers—some now have more than $1 billion in assets under management—and their numbers are growing rapidly.[2] They offer affluent clients comprehensive, integrated menus of services, including financial planning, investments, tax planning, estate planning, and much more. "Wealth management includes financial planning, but it's much broader in scope," said Tim Kochis, president of the San Francisco wealth-management firm Kochis Fitz and author of *Wealth Management: A Concise Guide to Financial Planning and Investment Management for Wealthy Clients*.[3]

> It includes implementation steps for the plan and particularly the management of investment portfolios all as part of a package. Ten years ago it was an avant-garde term. Now everyone uses it. I think eventually it will be considered the optimum service offering from the standpoint of the consumer.

Each wealth management firm sets a balance between the services on its own payroll and the services it refers to others, optimizing for the most successful and cost-effective client relationship. For a small wealth-management firm, referrals make good sense financially and strategically. If a client wants tax preparation, for example, a conscientious adviser doesn't hand over a list of accountants. Rather, he or she refers the work to an accountant while controlling and coordinating the relationship, stipulating that the accountant not solicit business from the advisory firm's clients without permission. The firm is able to expand its service menu without building another costly capability.

According to a benchmarking study of more than twelve hundred independent advisers performed in 2006 by Schwab Institutional, the wealth-management segment is growing at roughly the same rate as financial planning and money management, and large firms are growing at the same rate as small firms.[4] "What does vary," noted former Schwab Institutional president Deborah Doyle McWhinney, "is the growth rate of the fastest-growing firms." Those firms are growing at double the rate of their peers for three reasons, McWhinney said: they are well managed, with business strategies focused on a distinct group of target clients; they've built scale into their businesses, allowing them to grow efficiently; and they've built "a solid discipline around how they approach marketing and business development." The ability to focus on the needs of specific clients—whether it's wealth management, retirement planning, or investment consulting—is the most salient of the three factors, says McWhinney.

Accompanying the growing diversity of adviser types has been a wider range of investment offerings. Some advisers use a variety of actively managed funds, some use index funds, some use a single family of funds, and some use individual security portfolios tailored to the individual client. Other advisers are introducing an even wider variety of investment vehicles, including structured products, venture funds, real estate, or even insurance products.

Structured products have been an increasingly popular option, said Tom Winnick of DWS Scudder Mutual Funds, which provides such products to independent advisers. Structured products are hybrid investments that may combine a fixed-income return with an equity return from a derivative, such as an option based on a stock index or commodity index. Some include a fixed rate of return or other characteristics that make them attractive to certain types of investors. "Part of our job is to augment the product lineup of the independents so that they can provide the right solutions to their clients no matter how wealthy they may be," Winnick said. Jay Lanigan, former president of the Fidelity Registered Investment Advisor Group, said custodians have improved their ability to deliver such products to independent advisers. "They're now focused on upgrading their delivery of the whole gamut of alternative investments," Lanigan said. "The advisers are going to be able to offer anything that their larger competitors have in their product lines."

technology: the next generation

Beginning in the 1980s, powerful new technologies such as portfolio-management programs from Advent, Schwab Performance Technologies®, and other companies helped independent advisers enhance their services. Since then, continued advances in computational power have enabled them to keep improving their efficiency. Data aggregation, for example, allows advisers to consolidate client financial data from outside sources and to automatically generate complete financial statements with balance sheets and income statements. Customer relationship management systems help advisers stay in touch with clients, monitor workflow and quality control, and meet important deadlines. Paperless office technologies enable documents to be filed, stored, and retrieved electronically. "You're not necessarily seeing the death of paper yet," said Joel Bruckenstein, a consultant on adviser technology issues and the publisher of *Virtual Office News*, an industry newsletter. "But you are already starting to see a slow death of the copy machine, because in most cases today cutting-edge advisory firms are scanning everything into the system and if they need a copy they just print it."

No single technology development has been as influential as the Internet, which changed the way advisers accessed and used the technology itself. As services moved online they became cheaper and more flexible, scalable, and reliable. Broadband technology dramatically increased the speed of communications between independent advisers and their service providers. As a result, services delivered via the Internet moved well beyond basic desktop-computing services such as portfolio accounting and trade-order management that advisers had adopted in the early days of PCs. For example, Schwab and other service providers now use the Internet to deliver statements, trade confirmations, market research, prospectuses, and compliance and regulatory notices. Automated Internet-based systems also alert advisers to wire transfers of funds in and out of client accounts to satisfy client financial obligations.

"Today an adviser can't be in business without being on the Internet," said Bruckenstein. "Typically, advisers are now communicating with 80 to 90 percent of their clients at least occasionally by e-mail. Five years ago that number was as little as 25 percent."

Beyond e-mail and data transfer, some independent advisers are using online collaboration and Web conferencing technologies to provide personal service. Collaboration capability, built into some financial planning programs, allows two people to work on the same document from different locations. Web conferencing technology offers an efficient way to stay in contact with clients without having to travel to meetings.

Thanks to the Internet and 24-hour financial broadcasting, investors today have more access to market information than ever before. They expect their advisers to have similar access—and to act on it. As clients continue to demand that their advisers provide them with regular updates, advisers in turn will demand that service providers deliver information in real time, with customization options that allow greater flexibility for specific client requirements. Technology will play an increasingly important role in narrowing the gap between data and action, while at the same time allowing advisers to work more efficiently and profitably without adding extra staff.

the new face of retirement

Joel Bruckenstein's speculation is likely to become a certainty as technologically savvy baby boomers enter retirement. The 76 million people born between 1946 and 1964 currently control an estimated $15 trillion in assets.[5] The first wave of the biggest-ever generation will reach age 62 in 2008, and boomers will continue to enter retirement over the next two decades. Serving their financial needs will be big business, and advisers need to prepare, says Kurt Cerulli, president of the Boston financial services research firm Cerulli Associates.

> The issue on investors' minds is shifting from "How do I accumulate enough for retirement?" to "What do I do with it and how do I structure it properly so that I generate the income I need to live on?" Everyone is struggling with that issue, and independent advisers need to position themselves to offer those kinds of services. It's an area where they could do well

The first wave of baby boomers will reach 62 in 2008, and are looking to independent advisers to help with their complex retirement planning needs

because they're good at customized, personalized guidance and advice. They need to be positioned for those assets because that's where the growth is going to be.

The coming retirement boom represents both a challenge and opportunity for advisers. For one thing, retirement will be longer, riskier, and more complex for baby boomers than for previous generations. It's "uncharted waters," said David Hunt, managing director of the consulting firm McKinsey & Company—and not only because of "the demographic bulge":

> Retirement today is different because of the change in the structure of the retirement and pension system. The demographics simply underscore the change. We have seen a massive shift of risk from Social Security and defined-benefit pension plans to individuals and defined-contribution plans. And then there's the dramatic change in health care, both in government and in the reduced number of companies offering medical plans to their retirees. It adds up to a set of risks—investment risks, health care risks, inflation risk, and counter-party risk related to whether or not your defined benefit plan will survive—that my father, when he retired, couldn't have dreamed of.

The process of retirement has changed, too. No longer a single definitive moment that culminates with a handshake and a gold watch, it's more likely to be a gradual transition over several years, from full- to part-time employment and finally full retirement much later than the traditional age of sixty-five. Financial firms understand this trend but many have yet to adapt to it, a recent McKinsey study observed.

> They still operate under the old definition of retirement, with one set of options for workers and another for retirees. The new definition of retirement means people entering the transitional phase will have more complicated needs. This raises the bar substantially for advisers, if they are to become the credible, trusted financial guides that their clients will seek.[6]

Among those "more complicated needs" is the need to adjust investment goals from aggressive growth to risk mitigation. Investors' risk tolerance changes dramatically as they move from working life to retirement and begin to confront higher medical costs and the very real possibility of serious illness. Advisers can play an important role in protecting their clients from catastrophic risk during retirement.

This means independent advisers will be busier than ever in the decades to come. Without corporate pensions to support them, retired clients will need more advice about making good investment choices. "There's an inflection point when someone stops working," said Dale Yahnke of Dowling & Yahnke in San Diego.

> They've been getting W-2 income their whole life. They've done a great job of saving and they have enough money. But it's hard, psychologically, for people to stop working and say, "OK, I'm just going to passively take money out of my savings account." It's a tough barrier to get over. There are a lot of people who aren't very comfortable with that, even though they have enough money.

Post-retirement counseling is more complicated than advising clients during the years they are working and accumulating assets. Retirees need help calculating and managing mandatory withdrawals from retirement accounts and in making quarterly estimated tax payments. They may need reverse mortgages or income annuities, and they may want to make charitable gifts whose structure may require advisers to turn to outside specialists. Independent advisers may have to answer questions about Social Security, Medicare, long-term care insurance, and lifestyle options.

All these services represent a tremendous growth opportunity for independent advisers, said Deborah Doyle McWhinney. "The independent adviser industry is ideally poised to capture more and

"The new definition of retirement means people entering the transitional phase will have more complicated needs. This raises the bar substantially for advisers. . . "

—2006 MCKINSEY STUDY

more affluent investors," she said. "Not only are investors focusing more on retirement planning, but according to the McKinsey research, the next two generations of retirees are two to four times more likely than their parents were to use an adviser for retirement planning."

Along with the opportunity comes formidable challenges. For example, financial planners disagree about the maximum sustainable long-term withdrawal rate from investment portfolios. Some say it's 5 percent or more; others consider a 3 or 4 percent withdrawal rate to be safer. Better and more sophisticated tools for retirement income planning are clearly needed. A second challenge will come from clients who haven't saved enough during their working years to have a comfortable retirement. In addition, advisers will need to balance their retiree client base with younger clients to ensure consistent— and consistently growing—assets under management.

global expansion

The need to offer guidance to a large population on the brink of retirement isn't exclusively an American phenomenon. The independent adviser model is finding fervent advocates around the world, often in places that would have seemed improbable just a decade ago. In 2006, when the number of Certified Financial Planner (CFP) professionals topped 100,000 for the first time, half of those planners worked outside the United States. And the growth rate of CFP professionals is faster overseas than in the United States. "The trends that drove a lot of interest in financial planning in the United States are the same ones driving it around the world," said Noel Maye, chief executive of the Financial Planning Standards Board, which licenses Certified Financial Planner professionals outside the United States.

> Governments and employers [overseas] are moving away from guaranteed employment and guaranteed pension schemes. People are living longer and products and services are more complicated. The changes have made people realize, "We're going to be more personally responsible for our own financial future." So they need advice.

Nowhere has the shift from cradle-to-grave protection to individual responsibility been more striking than in China, where interest in

Worldwide CFP® certificant growth (1996–2006)

Date Affilliated	Country/ Region	1996	1997	1998	1999	2000	2001	2002	2003	2004	2005	2006
Dec-90	Australia	782	1,030	1,480	2,162	3,011	3,885	4,725	5,198	5,336	5,310	5,308
May-92	Japan	810	1,025	1,276	2,318	4,007	5,860	7,967	10,037	11,614	13,061	14,751
Jun-95	United Kingdom	60	63	80	131	190	215	232	284	400	510	610
Jan-96	Canada		4,700	6,900	10,677	11,850	13,277	14,483	15,492	15,928	16,350	16,834
Mar-96	New Zealand		265	268	226	240	253	268	287	307	346	385
Oct-97	Germany		23	227	349	451	601	694	880	921	973	1,009
Oct-97	France				172	283	540	850	1,200	1,297	1,433	1,471
Nov-98	South Africa				1,834	2,098	2,300	2,117	2,551	2,750	2,921	3,163
Dec-98	Singapore				3	3	91	212	370	505	539	548
Apr-99	Switzerland				99	140	239	280	287	287	235	242
Apr-00	Malaysia					9	24	961	2,580	2,320	2,581	2,689
Jun-00	Rep. of Korea						30	101	354	616	819	1,343
Nov-00	Hong Kong						88	334	996	1,422	1,929	2,293
Oct-01	India							0	0	54	90	134	235
Mar-02	Austria							19	54	82	88	110
Mar-02	Brazil							0	61	60	55	97
Jan-05	Chinese Taipei									0	148	345
May-06	China										0	488
Nov-06	Indonesia											0
Total FPSB Council		1,652	7,106	10,231	17,971	22,282	27,403	33,243	40,685	43,935	47,432	51,921
	United States	30,129	31,939	33,120	34,656	36,307	38,408	40,375	42,973	45,755	49,117	53,031
GRAND TOTAL		31,781	39,045	43,351	52,627	58,589	65,811	73,618	83,658	89,690	96,549	104,952

SOURCE: Financial Planning Standards Board

China's two stock exchanges, Shanghai and Shenzhen, list more than 1,200 companies and rival the Hong Kong Stock Exchange as Asia's second-largest stock market

professional financial planning services has exploded in the last few years. China's central government still exerts extraordinary influence: four state banks control 80 percent of the country's financial assets, and the country had no stock exchange between 1949 and 1990. Yet vigorous economic growth—10 percent a year for the last thirty years—has created a huge pool of new wealth and a corresponding demand for financial planning. In response, China started its first CFP certification training program in 2004, with three classes and 188 students. The following year 1,500 people enrolled; in 2006 that number grew to 10,000. And by the end of 2007, said Feng Liu, deputy secretary general of China's Financial Planning Standards Council, the number of CFP professionals in China will probably reach 2,000. The number of Associate Financial Planner certificants (the first level in the two-level CFP program) will reach 15,000. Most CFP professionals in China work for major banks, which have enthusiastically supported the financial planning movement. But the profession's expansion is constrained by a lack of qualified instructors for CFP certification-education classes. "The demand is so huge, if I had the capacity I could recruit 100,000 people for the program," Feng said. "But we want to maintain the quality of the program, so we need good instructors. Our other challenge is how to provide continuing education for licensed CFP professionals. What kind of content, and how do we organize this activity?"

Elsewhere, financial planning reflects national or regional histories and money-management styles (see "Tim Kochis: An Eye on Global Professionalism," page 119). Noel Maye of the Financial Planning Standards Board pointed to one development in nations where regulators look at standards of care:

> A lot of countries are benefiting from what we call supra-regulators, like the Financial Services Authority in the UK, or the monetary authorities in a lot of the Asian Pacific countries. Regulators there are able to take a more holistic view of the financial services marketplace. Regulators are taking an interest in the competency of financial practitioners and in ensuring that they treat customers and clients fairly. The regulators are saying, "It's not enough for you to say, 'I complied with the basic knowledge requirements' or, 'I complied with the basic licensing requirements' to either sell products or give advice. We're requiring a further level of care. How can you show you are

qualified to offer the advice you give or the services you provide? Was the product or advice you gave appropriate for that client situation, and if it was, how can you show me that it was? And firms are asking themselves, "How do we create a mechanism that gives rise to this culture of competency and treating customers fairly?" There's a very natural step there. And the regulatory environment is driving increased interest in financial planning.

That's less likely to be the case in the United States, Maye said, with its fractured regulatory scheme and focus on regulation of products. He added that this is an area where the U.S. advisory industry could learn from its overseas counterparts.

regulation from without and within

Regulation of independent advisers has worked remarkably well for the investing public since the passage of the Investment Advisers Act of 1940. Yet many advisers say the regulations governing them could work more effectively. "There's a deficiency in our regulatory scheme today," said Donald B. Trone, president of the Foundation for Fiduciary Studies in Pittsburgh.

> It's because we're still being regulated by a law that was written sixty-seven years ago. Sixty-seven years ago we had brokers who were executing transactions and selling financial products. And we had investment advisers who were money managers. The public knew the difference between the two and there wasn't any problem.

Since then, Trone said, the investing world has given rise to new types of advisers who are neither brokers nor money managers. For example, the Employee Retirement Income Security Act of 1974 (ERISA) helped create the investment consulting industry, which started in the pension fund world and has since branched out to serve private as well as institutional clients. "Unfortunately, though this industry now has been around for thirty-plus years," Trone said, "the NASD [National Association of Securities Dealers] and the SEC [Securities and Exchange Commission] haven't carved out an appropriate regulatory scheme for this new body of professionals."

> So we have brokers calling their folks financial advisers. We have wealth managers, we have financial consultants, we have trust

officers, we have financial planners. I would describe them all as people who are providing comprehensive and continuous investment advice. And there is no regulatory scheme that fits them.

There may be need for regulatory reform, but there has been no consensus within the industry or in Congress about what form it might take. A self-regulatory organization for investment advisers that might address some of Trone's concerns has found little support in Washington. And efforts to establish a specific regulatory framework for financial planners have so far been unsuccessful.

In contrast, industry initiatives such as professional certification and practice standards—for example, the Certified Financial Planner credential—have gained acceptance by some independent advisers, particularly those operating as financial planners. Such standards have helped improve the quality and consistency of financial advice. They also have helped independent advisory firms compete against representatives of banks and brokerage houses, who in the past had been slower to seek credentials such as the CFP mark, relying instead on their firms' brand names and institutional presence to attract clients.

As a result, there has been solid support over the years for enhancing professional standards. For example, the Certified Financial Planner Board of Standards, the governing body that oversees the CFP certification process in the United States, recently strengthened its practice standards. The new SEC proposal makes it clear that CFP professionals engaged in financial planning will be held to a fiduciary's duty of care. And the Pension Protection Act of 2006 imposes fiduciary obligations on firms offering advice to retirement plan participants.

Applying fiduciary standards to different types of clients requires skill and experience, says Donald B. Trone. "You have to develop a process for managing these decisions," he said. "And it doesn't make sense to have one process for 401(k) plans, another process for personal trusts, and a third for high-net-worth clients. Develop one process that's good for all of them."

Trone would also like to see stronger requirements for advisers' education and training. Most states require that advisers obtain only a Series 65 registration to become investment adviser representatives. "Barbers and beauticians today have higher education and training requirements than investment advisors," Trone pointed out. "If you study for fourteen hours you can pass the Series 65 exam and be fully qualified in the eyes of regulators to advise a 401(k) plan about its investment options or advise a university about managing its endowment." That's simply not good enough, Trone asserted.

the challenges ahead

Like members of any other thriving industry, independent advisers must avoid becoming victims of their own success. One consequence of rapid growth is the talent gap: a shortage of educated, experienced professionals to fill available positions at advisory firms. According to many advisers, finding qualified professionals is their number one issue. "There are lots of people capable of handling smaller clients," observed Steve Lockshin, chairman and chief executive officer of Convergent Wealth Advisors in Rockville, Maryland. "Finding people who can attract a wealthier and more sophisticated clientele is far more difficult." To groom a new generation of professionals, the adviser industry will need to work with colleges and universities to establish or expand their financial planning and wealth-management curriculum—something some trade groups in the adviser industry already have started to do.

Success has also bred imitators both large and small. Of the smaller competitors, Steve Lockshin observed that "there are a lot of people getting into this business, all dying for the next client, so they're killing themselves. They lower their fees to the point where they offer sub-par solutions and force other quality firms to lower their fees." Pricing, Lockshin said, "is one of the industry's biggest problems."

On the opposite end of the spectrum are large brokerage firms and banks that, until the 1990s, could afford to ignore independent advisers. No longer. To stay competitive, and in response to client demand, large national brokerage firms have been adopting the fee-based model of independent advisers. More attention was brought to this issue in 1999, when the SEC's Division of Investment Management, which directly regulates investment advisers and investment companies, provided "no-action relief" that enabled brokerage firms to offer fee-based accounts without triggering the Investment Advisers Act regulation. At the same time, the SEC proposed a rule, now known as the Merrill Rule, that allows brokerage firms to charge fees for advice that is non-discretionary and "incidental" to traditional broker-dealer services—such as custody, trade execution, and account maintenance—without registering as investment advisers under the Investment Advisers Act.

Between its proposal in 1999 and its adoption in April 2005, the Merrill Rule has been the subject of contention between broker-dealers who support it and investment advisers, financial planners, and others who oppose it. In protest, the Financial Planning Association filed a lawsuit against the SEC and scored a victory in March 2007, when the U.S. Court of Appeals for the District of Columbia Circuit ruled that the SEC had exceeded its authority in adopting the Merrill Rule.

In May 2007, the SEC indicated that it would not pursue an appeal of the federal appellate court's overturning of the Merrill Rule. Some industry observers believe that legislative intervention is the only answer to clarify the regulatory framework that exists in the converging broker-dealer and investment adviser space. "Congress probably will need to get into this fray to sort it out," said David G. Tittsworth, executive director of the Investment Adviser Association.

Meanwhile, the SEC is conducting a study with the RAND Corporation that will compare levels of protection afforded retail customers of financial service providers under the Securities Exchange Act and the Investment Advisers Act; the study will recommend ways to address investor protection concerns that arise from material differences between the two regulatory regimes.

"At a minimum," said Tittsworth, "the study should confirm what everyone already knows—that investors are very confused about the basic differences

> The adviser industry is working with colleges and universities to expand financial-planning curricula

DECEMBER 18, 2006

ONE ON ONE

Vicki Hampton of Texas Tech University

Ph.D. in family . Vicki Hampton get tenure at the tin in the mid-

been teaching a planning to non- ew to enjoy it so ancial planning e didn't get tenure ecome a certified

ut also got tenure er two passions. an academic pio- uting to financial writing research elines and bench- nancial well-being

also began writing ver-based Certified of Standards Inc.'s

oined the faculty of ubbock and, work- time friend Bill e school's financial nto one of the most

to become the first fer a Ph.D. program year. and has a real pas- nning," said Mr. f the program and ater for Financial ch. "And she always n the street. Other-

"probably not that lly being a financial aid. "You have this ple things that will n throughout their of feeling that, hey, nebody; I'm doing

um that Texas Tech ear so important?

we need to be edu- e at the undergrad- universities across at, you really need t the Ph.D. level to hat area.

ou expect in college ial planning for the

ot

ofessor and program

A. I would suspect we would see an annual growth rate of perhaps 10% or so for a good period of time. I think we are going to start seeing some major universities add programs. Currently, the programs are few and far between. A good goal would be if every state had two or three programs in them, which we don't have right now.

Q. Do you think that the demand is there from the industry side for qualified financial planners with a college degree? If so, what's driving it?

A. I think the demand is certainly there — like individuals making investment decisions in their 401(k) plans, the concern about Social Security, the large number of baby boomers reaching retirement and needing help, making their income last through retirement, not to mention those that haven't saved enough yet.

Q. Speaking of demographics, how important is it that financial planners themselves are a graying work force?

A. That's important, too. We see a lot of practitioners that come to interview our students that are looking for a succession plan. So, they'll get some reward for building the practice, but also their clients will be taken care of because they've trained a successor.

Q. What are the biggest challenges facing the growth of degree programs at the university level?

A. I think it's the resources to start a new program. It takes money to hire the faculty and to put something in place to start anything new. And most universities are not getting more resources. So they have to see this as being something that's the right thing to do. Universities that are losing enrollment are most likely to see this.

Q. Are CFPs and other practitioners making a persuasive case to colleges or universities?

A. I don't know that there's any big organized effort going on. We did receive some funding — a little less than $2 million — from the CFP Board in 2002 that was given to us over a seven-year period. And part of that mandate was to train Ph.D.s to go out and start new programs and add to existing programs.

Q. What else needs to be done to promote degree programs?

A. There's a lot that professionals can do to help programs grow. And some of it is as simple as just working with faculty and guest lecturing and mentoring students. Or it can get as complex as being part of advisory boards that help with development and raising money and professorships and grants and things of that nature.

> "Currently, the [degree programs for financial planning] are few and far between. A good goal would be if every state had two or three."

other people see that. So it's getting easier and easier. But we've got a long way to go yet.

Q. Why did you hire Deena Katz [president of ased Evensky & Katz

it less, partially because many of the academic programs are still at the point where they're just getting enough faculty to teach the base courses.

between investment advisers, brokers, and financial planners and the legal standards that apply to each."

Outside the courtrooms and the legislative chambers, industry insiders acknowledge that the competition is a sign of independent advisers' success. "One of the most flattering things independent advisers are seeing is how much their model, lingo, and practices are being imitated by other players in the advice-giving business," said Don Phillips, managing director of Morningstar. "It's the independent advisers who are writing the template for what financial advice is going to look like in the future."

David Hunt, managing director of McKinsey & Company, said he sees a growing convergence. "The large firms are increasingly taking a page out of the book of the independents," he said. It's not only fee-based pricing: Hunt says big firms are also building teams of fee-based brokers to serve clients as a group and stepping up local community-building and referral networks—both typical practices of entrepreneurial independent advisers.

Nevertheless, Deborah Doyle McWhinney said national brokerage firms will have a difficult time matching the kind of relationship independent advisers offer their clients.

> I'm constantly struck by the passion that independent advisers have for serving their clients and their insistence on doing what's right for them. It's a powerful experience for a client to work with an adviser who is sitting on the same side of the table with him or her. Clients really appreciate it. This isn't something that can be replicated overnight.

Most industry observers say national brokerages won't succeed in wooing away independent advisers' clients. "Competition is more of an issue in terms of bringing on a new client," said Tom Bradley, president of TD Ameritrade Institutional, a custodian and service provider to independent advisers. "It's highly unlikely that a large firm could introduce some advice service that could attract clients away from registered investment advisers, because they have such strong relationships."

Bradley and others also pointed to the continuing trend of "breakaway" brokers who leave large firms to start their own independent advisory businesses. In recent years, leading brokerages have encouraged the formation of teams of brokers who serve clients as a group.

TIM KOCHIS: AN EYE ON GLOBAL PROFESSIONALISM

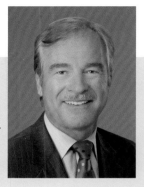

After more than thirty years in the financial planning profession, Tim Kochis could be excused if he chose to rest on his impressive laurels, which include the first Charles R. Schwab Impact Award™, given in 2006 for outstanding individual leadership in the independent advisory profession. Kochis also has been included in Worth magazine's list of the country's best financial advisers each year since the list was first published, in 1994. But taking it easy is the furthest thing from his mind. In addition to being the co-founder and CEO of Kochis Fitz, a prominent San Francisco wealth-management firm, Kochis—who earned a law degree and an MBA and ran financial planning practices at Bank of America and Deloitte & Touche before forming his own firm—devotes much of his time to improving professional standards both in the United States and abroad.

"The industry largely grew up while I've been participating in it," Kochis said. "When I started, there was no standard body of knowledge or standard of practice. We were building as we went along."

> "When I started, there was no standard body of knowledge or standard of practice. We were building as we went along."

A co-creator, at UCLA in 1980, of one of the first accredited financial planning programs in the United States, Kochis served for eleven years on the Certified Financial Planner Board of Standards and was chair of the body's board of examiners for five years. In that capacity he helped develop the CFP certification examination. Not long after, he began focusing on standards elsewhere in the world.

Recently, Kochis has chaired the Foundation for Financial Planning, the Financial Planning Standards Board, and the International Advisory Panel for the Financial Planning Standards Council of China. He says the development of financial planning in countries outside the United States has varied widely. "Canada and Australia are very much like the United States," he explained. "They have similar demographics and social expectations. It's not surprising that the development of financial planning in those countries has been similar to what it has been in the United States."

Japan presents a somewhat different picture, Kochis says. "There are a large number of financial planning professionals in Japan. The Japan Association for Financial Planning, for example, has more than 160,000 members. But the level of sophistication of financial planning in Japan is still largely focused on household-level financial planning, making sure you've got enough savings and insurance. Still, the Japanese are very disciplined about it, and they take financial planning at that level very seriously."

As for the European Union, Kochis said, "Europe offers sophisticated private banking for very wealthy people. But the broad availability of financial planning in Europe is limited and still emerging as people are just now beginning to recognize the need to plan their own financial affairs."

Throughout the world, Kochis says, one thing remains constant. "No matter where they live, people increasingly recognize the need to take responsibility for their financial well-being," Kochis said. "If we as a profession can be there to support their needs, that will be a wonderful accomplishment."

The team structure helps brokers specialize and provide better service to clients; it also makes it easier for them to leave as a group and start independent practices. The most important factor causing brokers to leave is the desire for a more autonomous and objective environment to serve their clients.[7] "Essentially, they're marketing themselves as advice givers," Bradley said.

> But they also are employed by large firms with investment banking arms that need their distribution capabilities. So how do you do both? How do you act as the fiduciary advice giver and also as your firm's salesperson? How do you always ensure that you're doing the right thing? It's a tough balancing act. And I think it has resulted in some dissatisfied stockbrokers who want to do the right thing for their clients, but don't like the position they're put in.

Are the big firms meeting the challenge of the independents? To some observers the answer is yes. Correctly or not, their offerings are often perceived to be comparable. According to the authors of the J. P. Morgan white paper:

> While what these organizations now provide to their clients may in many cases differ from that of independent advisory firms, it is hard for the uninformed client to differentiate the offerings. This factor combined with massive marketing and advertising budgets has made [national] and regional broker-dealers more effective competitors in certain markets.[8]

Here's a case in point: One of the authors of that study, Mark P. Hurley, is the former president of Undiscovered Managers, a mutual fund company. In 1999 Hurley wrote a controversial white paper, "The Future of the Financial Advisory Business and the Delivery of Advice to the Semi-affluent Investor," which predicted the advisory industry would consolidate as it matured, leaving a few big players, causing problems for smaller advisory firms. His firm was later acquired by JPMorgan Chase.

Consolidation is a fact of life in maturing industries, and the independent advisory industry is unlikely to be an exception. The principals of many firms are in their fifties or sixties; realizing their firms' value may be their best chance for a comfortable retirement. Other factors, such as rising costs and increased competition, may also persuade advisory firm owners to sell. Although they may prefer to sell to junior employees, they may not be able to: it can take five to ten years—or longer—to complete an internal sale, and many advisers wait too long to start the process. Once a firm reaches a certain size, it's almost impossible for employees to buy out the principals. An external sale may become the best—or only—option.

As J. P. Morgan Asset Management said in its 2005 white paper:

> We believe that the combination of increased business challenges, a graying owner population, the importance of the asset to funding these individuals' retirements and the long time period inherent in any transition has placed the industry at a tipping point. Over the next few years, many advisory firm owners will likely sell their firms. It will also lead to significant consolidation at the top of the industry.[9]

Not all industry observers concur. "There are some people who say all these small firms will all end up being rolled up into big national chains," said David Hunt of McKinsey.

> I've never been a particular buyer of that idea. I think there's something really special and unique about the small independently owned firms that are very focused on what they do. They do it well. They have strong relationships in the communities that they're in. Many of them don't want to work for a larger organization. It's one of their primary motivations. If you look at the motivation of the owner-practitioners it's not actually the type of people who want to work for larger organizations. So the notion that they're all going to be rolled up into large national chains I personally find very difficult to believe. The independent smaller owner operator has a very important role to play and will continue to be a very attractive option for many consumers.

If advisory firms do choose to sell, who will buy? "Banks have been reaching out and attempting to buy these [independent advisory] firms. And they've been willing to pay wonderful prices," said John Philip Coghlan, a former president of Schwab Institutional.

> In some cases it works out. In many cases instead it follows the model of banks trying to buy investment banking practices. After a short period of time, it doesn't fit with the way that those investment bankers served their clients in the past. So the principals go off and leave, and you try to reconstitute it in such a way that it works going forward.

One of the problems with banks and other large buyers, say some industry observers, is that the unique relationship between independent adviser and client is hard to replicate. Large firms that promise "personal" attention and "custom" plans may in fact be constrained by their business volume to provide standard offerings in several sizes. That's very different from the truly customized plans independent advisers have offered their clients. San Francisco executive Saul Feldman, a longtime client of an independent adviser, calls the adviser-client relationship a "holistic" approach, in his case one in which the adviser "understands my family situation, is responsive to my concern about socially responsible investments, and comes up with interesting ideas about what we ought to do going forward."

There's another option for some independent advisers who feel a need to sell yet want to retain their independence: selling to a holding company. One adviser who made that decision was Howard Sontag, founder and managing partner of Sontag Advisory in New York. After twenty years in the corporate world and ten years at the helm of his own firm, Sontag asked himself, "How is this business going to prosper going forward?" The answer took the form of an acquisition offer from National Financial Partners, a network of more than 175 independent firms, including several independent advisers. "In my business, I'm always telling clients to take money off the table when they have the opportunity to do so, and to strike a balance between fear and greed," Sontag said. "The offer from NFP allowed me to do exactly that, as well as create a clear succession plan and an exit strategy." Most important, the deal allowed Sontag Advisory to remain fully independent, with long-term management contracts. "As far as my clients are concerned, it's transparent," said Sontag. "It's as though the deal never happened."

Sontag's buyer, NFP, is one of several holding companies—others include Focus Financial Partners, Boston Private, Convergent, and WealthTrust—that have made multiple acquisitions of large advisory firms in recent years. Observers speculate that holding-company acquisitions may change the industry landscape, and not necessarily for the worse. Holding companies are generally committed to maintaining advisers' independence; they're more interested in maintaining cash flow—and eventually adding value and "recycling equity" to a successor generation—than in daily operations or decision making. When they evaluate potential acquisitions, they look for strong management teams that will continue to run their respective businesses.

There's another way to look at consolidation, says Mark Tibergien, a principal with the accounting and consulting firm Moss Adams, in Seattle. He believes mergers among peers will become an important trend. "Whenever a market is fragmented like this business is, there will be consolidators," he pointed out.

> But you're dealing with people who have feelings about control and other issues, and at an income level very different from that of, say, a funeral-home owner. These are people who are making serious money. And for them to cash out you're going to really have to get their attention. I think that the real consolidation is going to occur among like-minded advisory firms through mergers, as happened in the accounting profession, rather than having financial buyers be the players.

the road ahead

The independent advisory industry is nearly a century old, yet in real terms it's quite young. The majority of firms active today were founded within the past twenty-five years and are still under first-generation leadership. That means the industry is still very much an exciting work in progress, and its future over the next twenty years and beyond isn't easy to predict.

"I'll give you a ninety-five percent probability that our business will be unrecognizable in ten years," said Roger C. Hewins of Hewins Financial Advisors, a wealth management firm in Foster City, California.

> We're a national company, with headquarters in California, and thanks to technology it's no problem at all. Ten years ago we were getting big boxes of paper delivered. It's totally different now. It's a different business environment and there will be a lot of people who'll control a lot of wealth through computers—e-mail, instant messaging, the Web, maybe teleconferences with people in other parts of the world.
>
> What shape this industry will take is anybody's guess, but I can't help thinking it's got to become more efficient. That there's got to be more scale.

Deborah Doyle McWhinney echoed Hewins's speculation, saying that the most successful firms will make the smartest use of technology.

> You need to do all you can to automate functions so you can spend more time with clients. Firms that adopt technology are not only serving their clients and managing their businesses more efficiently, they're also growing more profitably.

Technology also allows easier entry into the independent adviser profession, noted Ken Fisher of Fisher Investments.

> You've got a computer, you've got some software, and you've got Internet access. It's easy to get a few clients. From there the question is, What do you do?

For Rick Keller, principal of the Keller Group Investment Management in Irvine, California, the answer to "What do you do?" is reflexive: it's all about building and maintaining relationships.

> It's not about the numbers. It's about the people. And it's about the relationship and who cares about you. I think our clients are with us because we care. You take good care of your clients, and they feel it.

Rich Steinberg of Steinberg Global Asset Management elaborated:

> We love helping people get from Point A to Point B. It may involve leaving money to charities, transferring wealth to the next generation, building financial security, reducing stress in their lives, helping widows or widowers, being a backstop when they have a problem, or even being like a family member. We had a client recently whose husband died and the kids live up in Boston. We were called in not to deal with the funeral arrangements but to work on everything else. And we don't get paid for that. It's just part of the relationship with that family that we developed over the years.

The challenges to the industry aren't trivial, as many advisers have pointed out; they include consolidation, competition, and succession issues. Yet since its inception in the second decade of the twentieth century, the independent adviser profession has proven to be remarkably flexible, innovative, and resilient. That's why many successful independent advisers today agreed with Tim Kochis of Kochis Fitz:

I don't see the future in terms of challenge. I see it in terms of opportunity and excitement. I'm as eager to get out of bed to get to work today as I ever was—maybe more so. I'm very enthused about the future of this business. I think it's going to become more sophisticated. I think we're going to do a better job for our clients. I think we have a very real opportunity to work with a manageable number of even more interesting clients over time. So the challenge, if there is one, is to continue to develop the skills and use the technology that will be necessary to respond to that opportunity.

But I have no doubt that we'll be able to do it.

These advisers' optimism and concern for "doing a better job for our clients" echo the prescient assertions of Arthur M. Clifford, Theodore Scudder, and other investment-advice pioneers. As Scudder's original partner, Haven Clark, put it, "[We] conceived the idea of starting a firm which would . . . advise clients how to invest money in an intelligent way." He added, almost as an afterthought: "The question was how to make any money out of it."

Nearly a century later, intelligent investment advice is still the most valuable product independent advisers offer, and their focus on the client remains center stage. And monetary success is no longer in question. An ever-expanding client base, ever-improving technology, and ever-higher professional standards have combined to make independent advisers one of the twenty-first century's pre-eminent providers of financial services. "Today's investors are increasingly looking for sound, individualized investment advice," says Charles Schwab, Chairman and Chief Executive Officer of The Charles Schwab Corporation. "When I think about the essential role independent advisers can play in the lives of their clients, I feel nothing but optimistic for the future."

1997	IAFP	Peggy M. Ruhlin, CFP®, CPA/PFS	Budros, Ruhlin & Roe, Inc.
1998	IAFP	G. Joseph Votava, Jr., Esq, CFP®, CPA/PFS	Nixon Peabody Financial Advisors, LLP
1998	ICFP	Robert J. Klosterman, CFP®, CLU, ChFC	White Oaks Wealth Advisors, Inc.
1999	ICFP	Elissa Buie, CFP®	Financial Planning Group, Inc.
1999	IAFP	Richard P. Rojeck, CFP®	Sagemark Consulting
2000	FPA	Roy T. Diliberto, CFP®, CLU, ChFC	RTD Financial Advisors, Inc.
2001	FPA	Guy Cumbie, CFP®	Cumbie Advisory Services
2002	FPA	Robert Barry, CFP®	Barry Capital Management, Inc.
2003	FPA	David Yeske, CFP®	Yeske Buie
2004	FPA	Elizabeth Jetton, CFP®	Mercer Global Advisors/Financial Vision
2005	FPA	James A. Barnash, CFP®	Ameriprise Financial
2006	FPA	Daniel B. Moisand, CFP®	Spraker, Fitzgerald, Tamayo & Moisand, LLC
2007-current	FPA	Nicholas A. Nicolette, CFP®	Sterling Financial Group

The National Association of Personal Financial Advisors (NAPFA) Board Chairpersons and Presidents 1983–2007

YEAR	PRESIDENT/CHAIRPERSON	COMPANY
1983	Gary Pittsford, President	Castle Advisory Group, LLC
1984/85	John Sestina, President/Chairperson	John E. Sestina 7 Company
1984	Gary Pittsford, Chairperson	Castle Advisory Group, LLC
1985/86	Michael Leonetti, President/Chairperson	Leonetti & Associates, Inc.
1986/87	Mary Malgoire, President/Chairperson	The Family Firm, Inc.
1987	Ron Meier, President	College for Financial Planning
1988	Gary Greenbaum, President	Greenbaum & Orecchio, Inc.
	Ron Meier, Chairperson	College for Financial Planning
1989	James Wilson, President	J. E. Wilson Advisors, LLC
	Robert Willard, Chairperson	Willard & Company
1990	Mike Kabarec, President	Kabarec Financial Advisors, Ltd
	Robert Willard, Chairperson	Willard & Company
1991	Greg Crawford, President	Crawford Financial Planning
	Don Wertheimer, Chairperson	
1992	Janet Briaud, President	Briaud Financial Planning, Inc.
	Peg Downey, Chairperson	Money Plans
1993	Robert Wacker, President	R. E. Wacker Associates, Inc.
	Janet Briaud, Chairperson	Briaud Financial Planning, Inc.
1994	Dave Diesslin, President	Diesslin & Associates, Inc.
	Robert Wacker, Chairperson	R. E. Wacker Associates, Inc.
1995	Andrew Hudick, President	Fee-Only Financial Planning, LLC
	Dave Diesslin, Chairperson	Diesslin & Associates, Inc.
1996	James Putnam, President	
	Mark Spangler, Chairperson	Spangler Financial Group, Inc.

1997	Carole Badger, *President*	
	Mark Spangler, *Chairperson*	Spangler Financial Group, Inc.
1998	Michael Chasnoff, *Chairperson*	Truepoint Capital
1999	Gary Schatsky, *Chairperson*	IFC Personal Money Manager, Inc.
2000	Gary Schatsky, *Chairperson*	IFC Personal Money Manager, Inc.
2001	Steve Kanaly, *Chairperson*	Kanaly Trust Company
2002	Steve Kanaly, *Chairperson*	Kanaly Trust Company
2003	Michael Joyce, *Chairperson*	JoycePayne Partners
2004	Jamie Milne, *Chairperson*	Milne Financial Planning, Inc.
2005	Peggy Cabaniss, *Chairperson*	HC Financial Advisors, Inc.
2006–current	Dick Bellmer, *Chairperson*	Deerfield Financial Advisors, Inc.

Investment Management Consultants Association (IMCA) Presidents 1985–2007

YEAR	PRESIDENT	COMPANY
1985–1986	John G. Brock	Robinson Humphrey Murphy
1987	George A. Dunn	E. F. Hutton & Company
1987–1988	Harold F. Rossen	Prudential-Bache Securities
1989–1990	Leonard G. Armstrong	Merrill Lynch
1991–1992	Robert B. Clelland	R. B. Clelland & Company
1993–1994	Victor P. Rosasco	Prudential Securities
1995–1996	Dale H. Stevens	Wurts, Johnson & Company
1997–1998	Elizabeth Weiner-Schulman	Merrill Lynch
1999–2001	F. Jeffrey Van Orden	Milliman & Robertson
2002–2003	J. Richard Joyner, *Co-President*	Ernst & Young
2002–2003	Peter Cieszko, *Co-President*	Citigroup
2004–2005	Norman E. Nabhan	Smith Barney Consulting Group
2006–current	Jeffrey B. Thomas	Raymond James Financial Services

Certified Financial Planner
Board of Standards, Inc. (CFP Board)
Chairpersons 1989–2007

YEAR	CHAIRPERSON	COMPANY
1989-1990	E. Denby Brandon, Jr., CFP®, CLU, ChFC	Brandon Financial Planning, Inc.
1991-1992	H. Oliver Welch, CFP®	
1993	Tom L. Potts, Ph.D., CFP®	Baylor University, Hankamer School of Business
1994	Bill E. Carter, CFP®	Carter Financial Management
1995	John T. Blankinship, Jr., CFP®	Blankinship & Foster
1995*	S. Timothy Kochis, CFP® (President)	Kochis Fitz
1996-1997	Donna G. Barwick, J.D., CFP®	Mellon Private Wealth Management
1998-1999	Harold R. Evensky, CFP®	Evensky Group
2000-2001	Patricia P. Houlihan, CFP®	Houlihan Financial Resource Group, Ltd.
2002	Elaine E. Bedel, CFP®	Bedel Financial Consulting, Inc.
2003	Fredrick E. "Rick" Adkins, CFP®	The Arkansas Financial Group, Inc.
2004	David H. Diesslin, MBA, CFP®	Diesslin & Associates, Inc.
2005	Glenn M. Pape, CFP®	Ernst & Young
2006	Barton C. Francis, CFP®, CPA/PFS, CIMA	PricewaterhouseCoopers
2007-current	Karen P. Schaeffer, CFP®	Schaeffer Financial

*Only year where CFP Board had both Chairperson and President positions

Financial Planning Standards Board (FPSB)
Chairpersons 2003–2007

YEAR	CHAIRPERSON	COMPANY
2003	John S. Carpenter	Certified General Accountants Association of Alberta (Canada)
2004	Maureen M. Tsu, CFP®	Professional Financial Advisors Inc. (United States)
2005	S. Timothy Kochis, CFP®	Kochis Fitz (United States)
2006	Elaine E. Bedel, CFP®	Bedel Financial Consulting, Inc. (United States)
2007	Margaret Koniuck, CFP®	CorporateCARE Inc. (Canada)
2007	Selwyn Feldman, CFP® Board Chairperson-elect	Old Mutual Actuaries and Consultants (South Africa)

Schwab Institutional
Advisory Board, 1995–2007

TENURE	NAME	COMPANY
1995	Nancy Abrams	Nancy Abrams & Associates
1995	Thomas P. Bellhy	Fort Pitt Capital Group
1995	Bruce Bower	Wealth Management, Inc.
1995	Jerome V. Bruni	J.V. Bruni & Company
1995	Jon S. Bull	Starbuck, Tisdale & Associates
1995	Donald F. Daly	Brundage, Story & Rose
1995	Harold Evensky	Evensky, Brown & Katz
1995	Mark Griege	Robertson, Griege & Thoele
1995	Edward M. Haberer	Cowgill-Harberer
1995	Mary A. Malgoire	Malgoire Drucker, Inc.
1995	Robert Markman	Markman Capital Management
1995	Timothy McCarthy	Van Deventer & Hoch
1995	David Petersen	Financial Services Advisory
1995	Jim Putman	Wealth Management, Inc.
1995	Dario Quiros	Hartford Financial Management, Inc.
1995	Stephen Rauh	Rauh, King & Kraus, Inc.
1995	Peggy M. Ruhlin	Budros & Ruhlin, Inc.
1995	Milton Stern	Bridgewater Advisors, Inc.
1995	Alfred M. Waddell	Waddell & Associates, Inc.
1995	Peter Westerlind, Ph.D.	Peter Westerlind & Associates, Inc.
1995	J. Harold Williams	Linscomb & Williams
1995	George Young	St. Denis J. Villere & Co.
1995-96	Michael H. Davis	Resource Consulting Group, Inc.
1995-96	William G. Hart	Hartline Investment Corporation
1995-96	Kenneth M. Heeter	Cornerstone Advisors, Inc.
1995-96	David E. Homrich	Homrich & Berg, Inc.
1995-96	Gregory C. Lathrop	Lathrop Investment Management Corporation
1995-96	Robert T. Lutts	Cabot Money Management
1995-96	Tom Lydon	Global Trends Investments, Inc.
1995-96	Brooks P. Nelson	Nelson Capital Management
1995-96	Judith A. Shine	Shine Investment Advisory Services
1995-96	Karen Spero	Spero-Smith Advisers, Inc.
1995-96	Morgan W. White	Woodside Asset Management
1995-96	Bruce Williams	L. Roy Papp & Associates
1995-96	Wayne Woodman	Tower Asset Management
1995-96	Dale Yahnke	Dowling & Yahnke
1996-97	Richard Bregman	MJB Asset Management, LLC
1996-97	James Brown	Independence Advisors, Inc.
1996-97	James Bruyette	Sullivan, Bruyette, Speros & Blayney, Inc.
1996-97	Malcolm Butler	Fiduciary Services Corporation
1996-97	P. Frank Castellon	MIIX Capital Mangement
1996-97	James Ferrare	Manchester Capital Corporation
1996-97	Andrew Goodwin, III	Graver, Bokhof, Goodwin & Sullivan, Inc.

1996-97	Jack Anderson	Howe and Rusling
1996-97	Mary Ann Greenwood	M.A. Greenwood & Associates, Inc.
1996-97	Kent Herr	Pritchard, Hubble & Herr, Inc.
1996-97	Lawrence Hood	Pacific Portfolio Consulting, L.P.
1996-97	Joel Javer	Sharkey, Howes, Wagner & Javer, Inc.
1996-97	Marr Leisure	Keller, Coad & Collins Investment Counsel, Inc.
1996-97	Fred Mitchell	Mitchell Capital Management Co.
1996-97	Christopher Morphy	Gamble, Jones, Holbrook & Bent
1996-97	Rajmiel Odinec	SOL Capital Management Company/Funds Management, Inc.
1996-97	Angela Parrish	Aon Investment Consulting
1996-97	J. Ronald Reid	International Research & Asset Management, Inc.
1996-97	Donald Mosby Rembert	Rembert, D'Orazio & Fox
1996-97	Mark Sievers	Sievers Financial Consultants
1996-97	Jeffery Stroman	Oxford Financial Advisors Corporation
1997-98	David Diesslin	Diesslin & Associates, Inc.
1997-98	Roy Diliberto	RTD Financial Advisors, Inc.
1997-98	Gene Dongieux	Mercer Global Advisors
1997-98	Kevin Malone	Greenrock Research, LLC
1997-98	Rolf Olson	Olson, Mobeck & Associates, Inc.
1997-98	John Scarborough	Bingham, Osborn & Scarborough, LLC
1997-98	Kenneth Schapiro	Condor Capital Management
1997-98	Gregory Schultz	Asset Allocation Advisors, Inc.
1997-98	Debra Silversmith	Sterling Partners
1997-98	Richard Sunshine	WHRS Investment Management
1997-98	Eddie Welch, Jr.	Welch, Hornsby & Welch
1998-99	Gregory J. Conway	Conway-Jarvis & Associates
1998-99	Mary C. Rinehart	Rinehart & Associates
1998-99	Hamilton P. Lewis, II	Hamilton Lewis Capital Management, Inc.
1998-99	Marilyn Capelli Dimitroff	Capelli Financial Services, Inc.
1998-99	Laura Tarbox	Tarbox Equity, Inc.
1998-99	Irwin S. Rothenberg	Wealth Management Consultants, LLC
1998-99	Joan M. Guccione	The BJ Group, Inc.
1998-99	Daniel L. Anderson	Pittenger & Anderson, Inc.
1998-99	Bruce C. White	Clifford Associates
1999-2000	Howard Alter	Alter Asset Management, Inc.
1999-2000	Walter Morales	Commonwealth Advisors, Inc.
1999-2000	David Vaughan	David Vaughan Investments, Inc.
1999-2000	Iris Mack Dayoub	Dayoub Financial Designs, Inc.
1999-2000	Katherine Banning Lintz	KBL Financial Management Partners
1999-2000	Sueanne M. Ramar	Nelson Capital Management
1999-2000	Norman M. Boone	Boone Financial Advisors, Inc.
1999-2000	William T. Baldwin	Pillar Financial Advisors
1999-2000	Edd H. Hyde	Radnor Financial Advisors, Inc.
1999-2000	Michael H. Davis	Resource Consulting Group, Inc.
1999-2000	P. Michael Sargent	Sargent Bickham & Associates, Inc.
1999-2000	Stewart H. Welch III	The Welch Group, LLC
2000-01	Ram Kolluri	GlobalValue Investors Inc.

2000-01	Neil Hokanson	Hokanson Capital Management
2000-01	Janet Miller	Rowland and Company Investment Counsel
2000-01	Sue McGrath	Vision Capital Management Inc.
2000-01	Bill Rankin	Stein Roe & Farnham
2000-01	Robert Bilkie	Sigma Investment Counselors
2000-01	Peter Mathieson	Guyasuta Investment Advisors, Inc.
2000-01	Ty Estlick	Windsor Financial Group
2000-01	Wayne Woodman	Tower Asset Management Corp.
2000-01	John Roberts	Denver Investment Advisors LL
2000-01	Tony Montag	A. Montag & Associates Inc.
2000-01	Mal Davis	R. M. Davis, Inc.
2001-02	Ronald Yolles	Yolles Investment Management
2001-02	Diahann Lassus	Lassus Wherley & Associates
2001-02	Ross Levin	Accredited Investors, Inc.
2001-02	Armond Dinverno	Dinverno & Foltz Financial Group
2001-02	Missy Kraus	M. Kraus & Company
2001-02	Mark Thomas	Old Dominion Capital Management Inc.
2001-02	Anne Golden	Montgomery Asset Management
2001-02	Susan Brewer	Cheswick Investment Co., Inc.
2002-03	Elaine Bedel	Bedel Financial Consulting, Inc.
2002-03	Susan Brewer	Cheswick Investment Co., Inc.
2002-03	James Dussold	Financial Advisory Services, Inc.
2002-03	Dan Genter	RNC Capital Management LLC
2002-03	Steve Holwerda	Ferguson Wellman Capital Management, Inc.
2002-03	Clayton Jackson	Zeliff Wallace Jackson Investment Counsel
2002-03	Chris Johnson	Capital Investment Council, Inc.
2002-03	Bob Palmer	Plante & Moran Family Wealth Advisors
2002-03	Gary Pollock	Bay Isle Financial
2002-03	Harold Williams	Linscomb & Williams, Inc.
2003-04	Stuart Danforth	The Danforth Associates
2003-04	Susan Freed	Susan Freed & Associates
2003-04	Roger Hewins	Hewins Financial Advisors
2003-04	Brian Keenan	Train, Babcock Advisors
2003-04	Joan Malloy	The St. Louis Trust Company
2003-04	Paul Muzzey	Capital Investment Services of America
2003-04	Steve Phelps	Badgley, Phelps and Bell
2003-04	Tom Plumb	Wisconsin Capital Management, Inc.
2003-04	Rich Steinberg	Steinberg Global Assets Management
2003-04	Ralph Walter	Kayne Anderson Rudnick Investment Mgmt
2003-04	George Young	St. Denis J. Villere & Co.
2004-05	Andy Berg	Homrich & Berg, Inc.
2004-05	Jeff Buckner	Plancorp, Inc.
2004-05	Susan Colpitts	Signature Financial Management
2004-05	David Henion	Forte Capital
2004-05	Roger Reynolds	Coldstream Capital Management
2004-05	Scott Roulston	Fairport Asset Management
2004-05	Drew Simon	Baydush Simon Weaver
2004-05	Marita Sullivan	JMG Financial Group
2004-05	Jon Vannice	Boys, Arnold and Company
2005-06	Andy Putterman	Lydian Wealth Management Co.

2005-06	Doug Lane	Douglas C. Lane & Associates
2005-06	Michael Yoshikami	YCMNET Advisors
2005-06	John Huber	Geneva Investment Management of Chicago
2005-06	Ann McCorkindale	Honkamp Krueger Financial Services
2005-06	Wendy Laidlaw	R.M. Davis Inc.
2005-06	Joel Isaacson	Joel Isaacson & Co.
2005-06	Libbie Agran	Libbie Agran Financial Services
2005-06	Lon Morton	Morton Capital Management
2005-06	Susan Spraker	Spraker Fitzgerald Tamayo
2005-06	Mark Griege	Robertson, Griege & Thoele
2006-07	Mark Homan	Diversified Management, Inc.
2006-07	Cheryl Holland	Abacus Planning Group
2006-07	Timothy Montague	Hamilton Capital Management, Inc.
2006-07	Douglas Kreps	Fort Pitt Capital Group, Inc
2006-07	Linda Davis-Taylor	Philip V. Swan & Associates
2006-07	Joseph Sheehan	Moneta Group, LLC
2006-07	Rich Simmonds	Laird Norton Tyee
2006-07	Bob Swift	TCI Financial Planning, Inc.
2006-07	Greg Thomas	ThomasPartners, Inc.

Notes

CHAPTER 1

1. S&P 500, the Standard & Poor's index. For a graph of the S&P 500 performance since 1950, see http://finance.yahoo.com/q/bc?s=%5EGSPC&t=my&l=on&z=l&q=l&c=.

2. Peter Schwartz, Peter Leyden, and Joel Hyatt, *The Long Boom: A Vision for the Coming Age of Prosperity* (Reading, MA: Perseus Books, 1999).

3. James K. Glassman and Kevin A. Hassett, *Dow 36,000: The New Strategy for Profiting from the Coming Rise in the Stock Market* (New York: Three Rivers Press, 1999).

4. Maggie Mahar, *Bull: A History of the Boom, 1982–1989* (New York: Harper-Collins, 2003) and John Cassidy, *Dot.con: The Greatest Story Ever Sold* (New York: HarperCollins, 2002), quoted in Brent Goldfarb, David Kirsch, and David A. Miller: "Was There Too Little Entry during the Dot Com Era?" Working Paper RHS-06-029 (University of Maryland, Robert H. Smith School of Business, April 2006).

5. McKinsey & Co., *Cracking the Consumer Retirement Code* (New York: 2006) 14; http://www.mckinsey.com/clientservice/bankingsecurities/latestthinking/retirement.asp.

6. Cerulli Associates, *The Cerulli Report: Retail Registered Investment Advisers in Transition* (Boston: 2004), 69 et seq.

7. Foundation for Fiduciary Studies, *Prudent Investment Practices: A Handbook for Investment Fiduciaries* (Pittsburgh, PA: 2004), 8.

CHAPTER 2

1. Scudder, Stevens & Clark, *The History of Scudder, Stevens & Clark* (New York: 1994), 7.

2. Charles R. Geisst, *Wall Street: A History: From Its Beginnings to the Fall of Enron* (New York: Oxford University Press, 2004), 151.

3. Herman Krooss, ed., *Documentary History of Money and Banking in the U.S.* (New York: Chelsea House, 1969), 2123.

4. Dwight Rogers, A Brief History of the Investment Counsel Association of America (New York: ICAA, 1982), p. 28.

5. Securities and Exchange Commission, Seventh Annual Report, U.S. Government Printing Office, 1942, page 34.

6. Kathleen M. McBride, "Standing Tall," *Investment Advisor*, October 2006, http://www.investmentadvisor.com/article.php?article=6838.

7. Rogers, *Brief History*, 6-7.

8. Loring C. Farwell, ed., *Financial Institutions* (Homewood, IL: Richard D. Irwin, 1966), 470.

9. Scudder, Stevens & Clark, *A History*, 24.

10. Senate Banking Committee, *Investment Trusts and Investment Companies: Hearings on S. 3580*, 76th Cong., 3d sess., 1940, 713.

11. Rogers, *Brief History*, 127.

12. U.S. Bureau of the Census, *Historical Statistics of the United States, Colonial Times to 1970*, Part 1, Series D 85-86, 135, quoted in Donald M. Fisk, "American

Labor in the 20th Century," *Compensation and Working Conditions*, Fall 2001, http://www.bls.gov/opub/cwc/cm20030124ar02p1.

13. Geisst, *Wall Street*, 174, 192.

14. Ron Chernow, *The House of Morgan: An American Banking Dynasty and the Evolution of the Modern Financial World* (New York: Atlantic Monthly Press, 1990), 353.

15. "Investment Investigation," *Time* magazine, August 10, 1936, http://www.time.com/time/magazine/article/0,9171,762313,00.html.

16. Ibid.

17. Senate Banking Committee, *Investment Trusts*, 765.

18. Scudder, Stevens & Clark, *A History*, 80.

19. Rogers, *Brief History*, VIII.

20. Senate Banking Committee, *Investment Trusts*, 1065.

21. Senate Banking Committee, *Investment Trusts*; and Rogers, *Brief History*, 711.

22. Senate Banking Committee, *Investment Trusts*, 765.

23. Rogers, *Brief History*, 37.

24. U.S. Securities and Exchange Commission, Division of Investment Management, "SEC 2000 Roundtable on Investment Adviser Regulatory Issues," May 23, 2000, http://www.sec.gov/divisions/investment/roundtable/iadvrndt.htm.

25. W. Scott Simon, "Fiduciary Focus: Non-fiduciary Investment Consultants (Part 4)," *Morningstar Advisor Edition*, August 31, 2006, http://advisor.morningstar.com/articles/doc.asp?docId=12353.

26. U.S. Securities and Exchange Commission, "History of the Investment Advisers Act," Appendix B of *Financial Planners: Report of the U.S. Securities and Exchange Commission to the House Committee on Energy and Commerce's Subcommittee on Telecommunications and Finance*, 1988, fn. 25, B-10.

CHAPTER 3

1. Geisst, *Wall Street*, 262 (see chap. 2, n. 2).

2. Rogers, *Brief History*, 55 (see chap. 2, n. 4).

3. Ibid., 57.

4. *SEC v. Capital Gains Research Bureau, Inc.*, 375 U.S. 1980 (1963).

5. Hugh F. Owens, "Investment Adviser Regulation: A Subject Too Long Neglected," *Financial Analysts Journal* 29, no. 1 (January-February 1973): 12.

6. U.S. Securities and Exchange Commission, "History of the Investment Advisers Act," Appendix A of *Financial Planners, Report of the U.S. Securities and Exchange Commission to the House Committee on Energy and Commerce's Subcommittee on Telecommunications and Finance*, 1988, fn. 73, A-17.

7. David G. Tittsworth, statement before the "SEC 2000 Roundtable on Investment Adviser Regulatory Issues," May 23, 2000, http://www.sec.gov/rules/other/f4-433/tittswo1.htm.

8. U.S. Securities and Exchange Commission, "Electronic Filing by Investment Advisers; Amendments to Form ADV" (effective October 10, 2000), http://www.sec.gov/rules/final/ia-1897.htm.

9. U.S. Securities and Exchange Commission, "Proxy Voting by Investment Advisers" (effective March 10, 2003), http://www.sec.gov/rules/final/ia-2106.htm.

10. U.S. Securities and Exchange Commission, "Custody of Funds or Securities of Clients by Investment Advisers" (effective November 5, 2003), http://www.sec.gov/rules/final/ia-2176.htm.

11. U.S. Securities and Exchange Commission, "Compliance Programs of Investment Companies and Investment Advisers" (effective February 5, 2004), http://www.sec.gov/rules/final/ia-2204.htm; and "Investment Adviser Codes of Ethics" (effective August 31, 2004), http://www.sec.gov/rules/final/ia-2256.htm.

12. Rich White, "A Preliminary History of the Organized Financial Planning Movement Part II: (1975–1979)," *The Financial Planner*, October 1979, 82.

13. E. Denby Brandon Jr., and H. Oliver Welch, *A History of the Financial Planning Movement: A White Paper* (Denver: Financial Planning Association, 2003), 9, http://www.fphistoryproject.org/fphistorywhitepaper_aug2003.pdf.

14. Rich White, "A Preliminary History of the Organized Financial Planning Movement Part I:-[1969-1974]," *The Financial Planner*, September 1979

15. S.S. Huebner and Kenneth Black, Jr., *Life Insurance*, tenth edition, Prentice-Hall, Inc., 1982 p. 22; and Mark S. Dorfman and Saul W. Adelman, *Life Insurance*, second edition, Dearborn Financial Publishing, 1992, p. 590

16. Rich White, "A Preliminary History of the Organized Financial Planning Movement Part I: (1969–1974)," *The Financial Planner*, September 1979, 17 et seq.

17. Gail Quint, ed., *Twenty Years of Excellence: A Look Back* (Denver: College for Financial Planning, 1992), 3.

18. Brandon and Welch, *History of Financial Planning*, 21.

19. Quint, *Twenty Years of Excellence*, 6.

20. Ibid., 9.

21. Ibid., 9.

22. Brandon and Welch, *History of Financial Planning*, 35.

CHAPTER 4

1. Loren Dunton, *The Financial Planner: A New Professional* (Chicago: Longman Group USA, 1986), 7.

2. Investment Company Institute, *Mutual Fund Fact Book 1997* (Washington, DC), 19.

3. J. Bradford De Long, *America's Only Peacetime Inflation: The 1970s*, National Bureau of Economic Research Paper No. 84 (Cambridge, MA: 1996), 2.

4. August C. Hansch, *Controlling Tomorrow* (Rockville Centre, NY: Farnsworth Publishing, 1980), 68–72.

5. Internal Revenue Service, *Legislative History of Abusive Tax Shelters* (Washington, DC: GPO, n.d.) 1, http://www.irs.gov/pub/irs-utl/i.b_-_history_of_shelters.pdf.

6. Investment Company Institute, *Mutual Fund Fact Book* (Washington, DC: 1992, 2004).

7. Bruce R. Bent, chairman of The Reserve Funds, in "Wall Street Museum Honors Bruce Bent and Celebrates a Milestone in Financial History," a statement issued October 8, 2001, on the 30th anniversary of the launch of the money market mutual fund.

8. Mary Rowland, *The Fidelity Guide to Mutual Funds* (New York: Simon & Schuster, 1990), 35.

9. "Prosperity Blunts 'Mayday's' Edge, *Time*, April 18, 1975.

10. Employee Benefit Research Institute, *Retirement Plans for the Self-Employed*, Section 17 (Washington, DC, n.d.), http://www.ebri.org/pdf/publications/books/fundamentals/fund17.pdf.

11. John B. Keeble III, "The Race to Capture Assets: Will Insurance Companies Emerge Victorious?" *Journal of Financial Planning*, August 2000, http://www.fpanet.org/journal/articles/2000_issues/jfp0800-art14.cfm.

12. Rich White, "A Preliminary History of the Organized Financial Planning Movement Part I (1969–1974)," *The Financial Planner*, September 1979, 21.

13. E. Denby Brandon Jr., and H. Oliver Welch, *A History of the Financial Planning Movement: A White Paper* (Denver: Financial Planning Association, 2003), 11, http://www.fphistoryproject.org/fphistorywhitepaper_aug2003.pdf.

14. Sarah Holden, et al., *The Individual Retirement Account at Age 30: A Retrospective*, (Washington, DC: Investment Company Institute, 2005), 4.

CHAPTER 5

1. "The 36¢ Buck Stops Here," *Time*, Feb. 16, 1981.

2. Quotes are from Markowitz's autobiographical statement on the Nobel Prize Web site, http://nobelprize.org/nobel_prizes/economics/laureates/1990/markowitz-autobio.html.

3. U.S. Securities and Exchange Commission, *Financial Planners: Report of the U.S. Securities and Exchange Commission to the House Committee on Energy and Commerce's Subcommittee on Telecommunications and Finance* (Washington, DC: 1988), 7.

4. Ibid.

CHAPTER 6

1. Sharon J. Weinberg, Mark P. Hurley, et al., *Back to the Future: The Continuing Evolution of the Financial Advisory Business*, (J. P. Morgan Asset Management: New York, 2005).

2. Cerulli Associates, *The Cerulli Report: Retail Registered Investment Advisers in Transition* (Boston: 2004), 95.

3. 2nd ed. (Chicago: CCH, 2006).

4. Schwab Institutional, *RIA Benchmarking: Growth Trends Study* (San Francisco: 2006).

5. McKinsey & Co., *Cracking the Consumer Retirement Code* (New York: 2006), 2, http://www.mckinsey.com/clientservice/bankingsecurities/latestthinking/retirement.asp.

6. McKinsey & Co., *The Retirement Journey: Pathways to Success in the New Retirement Market* (New York: 2005), 13, http://www.mckinsey.com/clientservice/bankingsecurities/latestthinking/The_Retirement_Journey.pdf.

7. Cerulli Associates, *Cerulli Report*, 118.

8. Weinberg, Hurley, et al., *Back to the Future*.

9. Ibid.

Photo Credits

Pp i, ii–iii: *Bronze Star* by Howard Jones, © Albright-Knox Art Gallery/CORBIS

CHAPTER ONE

Pp xviii, 1: © REUTERS/Scott Olson: p 2: © Chris Hondros/Newsmakers; p 3: TIME Magazine, © 1999, Time Inc. Reprinted by permission; p 7: Courtesy Morningstar, Inc.; p 12: © REUTERS/Ray Stubblebine; p 13: Courtesy Securities and Exchange Commission; p 14: Charles Schwab & Co., Inc.

CHAPTER TWO

Pp 16, 17: © Bettmann/CORBIS; p 18: The 16th Amendment, March 15, 1913; Ratified Amendments, 1795-1992; General Records of the United States Government; Record Group 11; p 19: top, © Bettmann/CORBIS; bottom, Library of Congress, Prints & Photographs Division, WWI Posters, LC-USZC4-9054; p 20: Harvard College Library; p 24: Hulton Archive/Getty Images; p 25: top, © Bettmann/CORBIS; bottom, © Underwood & Underwood/CORBIS; p 26: top, TIME Magazine, © 1933, Time Inc. Reprinted by permission; bottom, © Bettmann/CORBIS ; p 27: © Bettmann/CORBIS; p 28: © Bettmann/CORBIS; p 29: Courtesy Investment Adviser Association; p 30: Courtesy Investment Adviser Association; p 33: Edwin Merrick Dodd, 1941. Photograph by Louis Fabian Bachrach (1881–1963), copyright by Louis Fabian Bachrach, used by permission. Courtesy of Special Collections Department, Harvard Law School Library; p 34: © Bettmann/CORBIS; p 36: Courtesy Investment Adviser Association

CHAPTER THREE

Pp 38, 39: © Bettmann/CORBIS; p 40: top, © Bettmann/CORBIS; bottom, "TIME Magazine, © 1938, Time Inc. Reprinted by permission.; p 43: © CORBIS; p 44: © Bettmann/CORBIS; p 45: © Eric Freeland/Corbis SABA; p 46: www.sechistorical.org, The Virtual Museum and Archive of SEC and Securities History; p 47: top, Courtesy Securities and Exchange Commission; bottom, www.sechistorical.org, The Virtual Museum and Archive of SEC and Securities History; p 49: Courtesy College for Financial Planning; p 53: Courtesy College for Financial Planning; p 54: Courtesy College for Financial Planning; p 55: www.sechistorical.org, The Virtual Museum and Archive of SEC and Securities History

CHAPTER FOUR

Pp 56, 57: © Bettmann/CORBIS; p 58: © Bettmann/Corbis; p 59 © Bettmann/CORBIS; p 60: © Bettmann/CORBIS; p 62: © Bettmann/CORBIS; p 65: © Alen MacWeeney/CORBIS; p 66: © The New York Times, originally published January 7, 1973; p 68: © The New York Times, originally published May 1, 1975; p 69: The Bancroft Library, University of California, Berkeley; p 70: Brooklyn College Library Archives; p 73: Courtesy Morningstar, Inc.

CHAPTER FIVE

Pp 76, 77: © Bettmann/CORBIS ; p 78: TIME Magazine, © 1986, Time Inc. Reprinted by permission.; p 79: © IBM/Handout/epa/Corbis ; p 81: Courtesy Advent Software, Inc.; p 83: © CORBIS; p 84: Courtesy of Mark J. Machina, Department of Economics, University of California, San Diego; p 88: © Bettmann/CORBIS; p 89: Charles Schwab & Co., Inc.; p 92: Charles Schwab & Co., Inc.; p 94: Courtesy Moneta Group, LLC

CHAPTER SIX

Pp 98, 99: © Damon Winter/Dallas Morning News/Corbis; p 100: © Greg Smith/Corbis; p 101: © REUTERS/Peter Morgan; p 108: © Getty Images; p 112: © REUTERS/Claro Cortes; p 117: Courtesy InvestmentNews, December 18, 2006. © Crain Communications, Inc. Photo of Vickie Hampton, © Robert Suddarth Photography; p 119: Courtesy Kochis Fitz

TIMELINE

P 127: (top to bottom) Detlev van Ravenswaay / Photo Researchers, Inc; SSA History Archives; Photo Researchers; Library of Congress photo, LC-US262-123278. P 128: (top to bottom) Corbis; Corbis; Bruce Roberts / Photo Researchers, Inc.; Photo Researchers; Getty Images; Courtesy of the College for Financial Planning; White House photo. SSA History Archives. P 129: (top to bottom) Reuters; Corbis; Getty Images

Index

IAFP (International Association for Financial Planning), 49–50, 70
ICAA (Investment Counsel Association of America), 23, 30, 35, 41. *See also* IAA (Investment Adviser Association).
IDS Corporation, 55
income tax authorization, 18
independent adviser profession
    conflicts of interest, 22–23
    consolidation, 116–123
    future challenges, 116–125
    growth of
        1945 - today, 47–55
        1950s - 1970s, 42–47
        background, 17–21
        Great Depression, 24–28
        pioneers, 21–23
        post-9/11, 101–106
        World War II, 39–42
    professional practices. *See* legislation; regulation.
    regulation. *See* investigations; legislation; regulation.
    small firms *versus* large, 116–123
independent advisers
    See also financial planning
    See also money management
    See also wealth managers
    client focus, 8–11
    definition, 3
    demographics, 10
    fiduciary role, 13
    innovation, 7–8
    investment counselors *versus* investment advisers, 30
    risk coaching, 8–11
    services, 3–6
Individual Retirement Account (IRA), 70
inflation
    1970s, 59–60
    an insidious thief, 59–60
    stagflation, 57
insidious thief, 59-60
Insull, Samuel, 26
International Association for Financial Counseling. *See* IAFP (International Association for Financial Planning).
International Association for Financial Planning (IAFP). *See* IAFP (International Association for Financial Planning).
investigations. *See also* legislation; regulation.
    depression era, 25–28
    mutual funds, 29
    nondisclosure, 43–45
Investment Adviser Association. *See* IAA (Investment Adviser Association).
Investment Advisers Act (1940). *See also*

National Securities Markets Improvements.
    amendment, 46, 48
    enactment, 34
    success of, 35–36
Investment Advisers Supervision Coordination Act, 48
Investment Company Act (1940), 34
Investment Company Institute, 67
investment counselors *versus* investment advisers, 30. *See also* independent advisers.
investment planners. *See also* independent advisers.
    demographics, 10
    versus investment counselors, 30
    SRO (self-regulatory organization), 46
Investors Economic Services, 22
IRA (Individual Retirement Account), 70

J

J. P. Morgan and Company, 26, 120
J. P. Morgan Asset Management, 103, 121
Jack White & Co., 92
Japan Association for Financial Planning, 119
Johnson, Lyndon, 47, 59
Johnston, Douglas T., 32
Johnston, James R., 49–50, 53, 55
Johnston & Lagerquist, 32
JPMorgan Chase, 120

K

Kahneman, Daniel, 11–12
Katz, Deena, 9
Kearns, Lewis G., 53
Keeble, John B., III, 69
Keller, Rick, 81, 124
Keller Group Investment Management, 124
The Keller Group Investment Management, 81
Kennedy, Joseph P., Sr., 28
Keogh, Eugene J., 69–70
Keogh plans, 69
Kochis, Tim, 104, 119, 124
Kochis Fitz, 104, 119, 124
Koopmans, Tjalling, 84

L

Lane, Doug, 104
Lanigan, Jay, 92, 105–106
Laurence Booth & Company, 22
Leemon, Dan, 78
legislation. *See also* investigations; regulation.
    Clayton Antitrust Act (1914), 18
    conflict of interest, 36

depression-era reform, 34
Federal Reserve Act, 18
full disclosure requirements, 35
Glass-Steagall Act (1933), 34
income tax authorization, 18
Investment Advisers Act (1940). *See also* National Securities Markets Improvements.
    amendment, 46, 48
    enactment, 34
    success of, 35–36
Investment Advisers Supervision Coordination Act, 48
Investment Company Act (1940), 34
Maloney Act (1938), 34
National Securities Markets Improvements, 48. *See also* Investment Advisers Act (1940).
need for, SEC report on, 32–35
Public Utility Holding Company Act (1935), 18, 34
registration of investment counselors, 35
SEC authority, 35–36
Securities Act (1933), 34
Sixteenth Amendment, 18
Tax Reform Act (1969), 57
Tax Reform Act (1976), 62
Tax Reform Act (1986), 62
Lockshin, Steve, 116
Loring, Augustus P., Jr., 32
Lydian Wealth Management, 116

M

Macklin, Gordon S., 54
Malgoire, Mary A., 86, 89
Maloney Act (1938), 34
Mansueto, Joe, 73
Marketplace, 85, 87
Markowitz, Harry, 84
Marschak, Jacob, 84
Martin, William McChesney, 39–40
Maye, Noel, 110, 113–114
McGonigle, John, 85, 91–92
McKinsey & Co., 5–6, 71, 108–110, 118, 121
McWhinney, Deborah Doyle, 105, 109, 118, 124
Microsoft, 1
Miller, Merton H., 84
Mitchell, Charles, 18, 26
Moneta Group Investment Advisors, 94, 96
money management. *See also* independent advisers.
    computerized, 93–96
    demographics, 10
    description, 101–102
money market funds, 63–68. *See also* mutual funds; tax shelters.